MW01093925

LIVING WITH PURPOSE BIBLE STUDY

Psalms

LIVING WITH PURPOSE BIBLE STUDY

Psalms

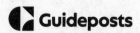

A Gift from Guideposts

Thank you for your purchase! We want to express our gratitude for your support with a special gift just for you.

Dive into *Spirit Lifters*, a complimentary e-book that will fortify your faith, offering solace during challenging moments. Its 31 carefully selected scripture verses will soothe and uplift your soul.

Please use the QR code or go to **guideposts.org/ spiritlifters** to download.

Living with Purpose Bible Study: Psalms

Published by Guideposts
100 Reserve Road, Suite E200
Danbury, CT 06810
Guideposts.org

Cover design by Judy Ross
Interior design by Judy Ross
Cover photo by bauwimauwi/iStock
Typeset by Aptara, Inc.

ISBN 978-1-961251-28-1 (hardcover)
ISBN 978-1-961251-29-8 (softcover)
ISBN 978-1-961251-30-4 (epub)

Printed and bound in the United States of America
10 9 8 7 6 5 4 3 2 1

CONTENTS

About Living with Purpose Bible Study

For as long as humankind has existed, we have pondered our place in the universe. Poets and preachers, philosophers and scientists alike have explored the topic for generations. Our busy modern lives leave little time for contemplation, and yet we move through our lives with nagging questions in the back of our minds: *Why am I here? What am I meant to do with my life?*

Fyodor Dostoevsky wrote that the "mystery of human existence lies not in just staying alive, but in finding something to live for." You might wonder how living with purpose ties in with the Bible. That's because God's Word is a guidebook for life, and God Himself has a purpose—a unique mission—for and unique to you. Reading the Bible and seeking God through prayer are two of the main ways God speaks to people. And when we begin to seek God, when we pursue His truth, when we begin to live our lives in ways that reflect His love back to others, we begin to find that purpose. Finding our purpose is not a destination; it is a journey we'll travel until we leave this earth behind and go to our heavenly Father.

Most of us know something about the Bible. We might be able to quote verses that we memorized as kids. Many of us have read parts of it, have learned about it in Sunday school both as children and adults. But not as many of us *know* the Bible, and that is where this Bible study comes in.

"Bible study" is a term that can elicit a variety of responses. For some people, the feeling that comes is a daunting sense of intimidation, even fear, because we worry that the Bible will somehow find us wanting, less than, rejected. Maybe we've heard preachers wielding the Bible as a weapon, using it as a measuring rod and a dividing line that separates "us" from "them."

Guideposts' *Living with Purpose Bible Study* addresses these questions and concerns with a hope-filled, welcoming, inclusive voice, like the one you've grown to know and love from Guideposts' devotional books, story collections, magazines, and website.

Best of all, you'll discover that the writers of *Living with Purpose Bible Study* are experts not only in the depth of their Bible knowledge but also in sharing that knowledge in such a welcoming, winning way that you can't help but be drawn in.

The writers come alongside you as trusted friends, guiding you through each volume in that warm, inviting manner that only Guideposts could bring you.

Each volume in the study draws from five trusted translations of the Bible: the New International Version, New American Standard Bible, the Amplified Version, the English Standard Version, and the King James Version of the Bible. We encourage you to keep your favorite Bible translation on hand as you read each study chapter. The Bible passages you read act as the foundation from which the study writer's insights, information, and inspiration flow. You can read along with the writers as each chapter unfolds, or you can read all of the passages or verses included in the chapter prior to reading it. It's up to you; you can use the method that works best for you.

In addition, you'll find two distinct features to enhance your experience: "A Closer Look" entries bring context by presenting historical, geographical, or cultural information, and "Inspiration from Psalms" entries demonstrate the spiritual insights people like you have gained from their knowledge of the biblical text. We've also provided lined writing spaces at the end of each lesson for you to jot down your own thoughts, questions, discoveries, and *aha* moments that happen as you read and study.

A final note: before you read each chapter, we encourage you to pray, asking that God will open your eyes and heart to what He has to say. Our prayer for you is that you find a new or renewed sense of purpose and grow closer to God as you deepen your understanding of God's Word by enjoying this *Living with Purpose Bible Study*.

—*The Editors of Guideposts*

An Overview of Psalms

T he very size of the book of Psalms is intimidating to many people. What other book of the Bible has 150 chapters? But, unlike most other Bible books, it is not something we need to read from beginning to end for it to make sense. Indeed, many of the psalms may be read one at a time without any concern for order, for there is little attempt in the book of Psalms to group them thematically or chronologically.

We won't be covering all the psalms—such a study would be much longer than this one. Instead, we'll be immersing ourselves in an overview of the psalms—their structure, their categories, the cultural background from which they arose, and more—using carefully selected psalms that will help us see the big picture and give us a much better foundation when we read the rest of the psalms.

The psalms are the lyrics of the worship music of Israel in the ancient tabernacle and temple periods. We have scant information and understanding of the forms of the music itself, but we do have the words.

The book of Psalms, then, is an anthology of the worship texts of ancient Israel. We will begin our journey in Psalms by clustering together those of similar type or content. And by coming to know something of these various types, we will then be prepared to read with understanding many other psalms that are similar.

Guidelines

There are some helpful things to know before we begin our journey in the book of Psalms. In our study we will note six factors that are particularly striking: (1) Hebrew language, (2) Hebrew poetry, (3) Canaanite culture, (4) forms and patterns, (5) authorship, and (6) God in the psalms.

Hebrew Language

First, the psalms are written in the Hebrew language. In fact, all the Old Testament was written in Hebrew, except for some small sections of the book of Ezra and a section of the book of Daniel, which were written in Aramaic and a few words in Greek. Aramaic was a language related to biblical Hebrew.

The Hebrew language is different from English in that it centers on the verb. Most verbs are made of three-consonant letter clusters. For example, the letters *m-l-k* convey the idea "to rule" or "to be king." The addition of vowels and other letters will modify and make more specific the general idea of the verbal root.

Therefore, we can spell our word *m-l-k* as *malak*, to mean "he ruled," *yimlak*, to mean "he will rule," *malkut*, to mean "kingdom," or perhaps *melek*, to mean "king." The verb-centered nature of Hebrew makes it a language that is particularly graphic and action-centered. Hebrew style is given to pictorial descriptions. It is a language ideally suited to poetic and narrative use. But one perceived weakness in biblical Hebrew is in the time of the action of the verb. Hebrew verbs center on kind of action rather than time of action.

This means that the time-centered nature of English makes demands on the translator that are not easily met.

Hebrew Poetry

Second, the psalms were written as Hebrew poetry. Therefore, even when we read these poems in an English translation, it will be helpful to know something about the style of Hebrew poetry. In one sense, Hebrew poetry shares certain basic elements with poetry the world over. Poetry is the language of experience, feeling, and emotion. And it is the most concentrated of all language forms, meaning that poetry packs a lot into a short, succinct package. Poetry has a high concentration of figurative language, sensory terms, and pictorial images. Hebrew poetry shares all of these features.

But there is something unusual to us in Hebrew poetry and that is the way one line of the poem relates to the next. Hebrew poetry is not based on rhyme or rhythm, as is much of Western poetry. While there is a rhythm in the words of a Hebrew poem, it does not have a predictable rhythm. There may be rhymes from time to time, along with assonance (repetition or echoes) and alliteration. But these are unexpected, unusual, and unnecessary for Hebrew poetry.

Because the poetry of the Bible follows these surprising turns, it was not until early modern times that the true genius of Hebrew poetry was discovered. This great discovery was made by Bishop Robert Lowth, professor of poetry at Oxford University, in 1763. Bishop Lowth discovered that the essential feature of the poetry of the Bible is the repetition of an idea by means of restatement and refinement. This he called parallelism.

Lowth, and others who followed him, described three types of parallelism that we may illustrate using familiar verses from the first Psalm.

- *Synonymous parallelism,* where the two lines say nearly the same thing. As you read the words, you will see that these lines are not just repetition—they involve a creative restatement of a similar idea:
  "But his delight is in the law of the LORD, and on his law he meditates day and night" (1:2, ESV).
- *Antithetical parallelism,* where the two lines make their point by contrasting elements. As you read these words, you will notice how the elements interplay with each other for a more comprehensive idea:
  "For the LORD knows the way of the righteous, but the way of the wicked will perish" (1:6, NASB).
- *Synthetic parallelism,* where the two lines are roughly synonymous but where the second (or third) advances the idea of the first. As you read these words, you may see a gradual development of intensity:
  "Blessed is the man who walks not in the counsel of the wicked, nor stands in the way of sinners, nor sits in the seat of scoffers" (1:1, ESV).

Contemporary scholars debate over how to revise or refine their descriptions of parallelism in the psalms. But the descriptions we have listed here have been the accepted ones for over 300 years.

Canaanite Culture

A third essential guideline in the reading of the book of Psalms is to be prepared for many examples of literary allusions from the Canaanite culture that preceded Israel in the Land of Promise. This does not mean that the poets who wrote these psalms were adapting Canaanite ideas into the true religion of the God of Israel. But as they spoke and wrote, they did so in a cultural context that was rich with images that they adopted for their own uses.

For example, as we read the psalms, it is helpful to know that the sea conveyed to these ancient poets something quite different from what we might imagine today. For us, mention of the sea might evoke images of power, adventure, distant ports, and exotic lands. But, for the writers of the psalms, drawing on Canaanite imagery, the sea was a picture of evil power, a malevolent force. In Canaanite mythology, the sea was a deity, the god Yamm. Now, the writers of the psalms never believed that the sea was a god, but the image of the sea often serves as a convenient way to depict an enemy of God. This accounts for the unusual wording of Psalm 93:4: "Mightier than the thunder of the great waters, mightier than the breakers of the sea—the LORD on high is mighty" (NIV).

From time to time, we shall observe other Canaanite imagery in the psalms. Our understanding of these features comes primarily from the study of a collection of Canaanite literature discovered in 1929 at the ancient site of Ugarit (modern Ras Shamra) in coastal northern Syria. The poetic, mythological texts from Ugarit have an immense bearing on the poetic ideas that the Psalmists present.

Forms and Patterns

Yet another aspect of psalms research that has greatly enhanced our understanding of them is the development of a branch of scholarship called form criticism. While we might bristle at applying the word *criticism* to the Bible, in the context of biblical studies, it doesn't mean attacking, denigrating, or finding fault with. In his book *Christian Theology*, respected Bible teacher Millard Erickson described form criticism as "the endeavor to get behind the written sources of the Bible to the period of oral tradition, and to isolate the oral forms that went into the written sources." At its basic level, the ideas of form criticism are quite simple. There are patterns in literature that serve as models for doing certain types of writing, just as there are forms and patterns in contemporary artistic and popular culture.

Think of television, for example. No one who has grown up in the last 60 years needs to be told that there are forms in television programming. No one would confuse the pattern—the format—of a daytime talk show with a reality show, or the format of a crime drama with that of a late-night talk show. All of art, music, and literature is filled with forms and patterns, as is all of life.

It was only in the opening years of the twentieth century, however, that the forms and patterns of the psalms were described and analyzed. Today, Bible scholars expend great energy in classifying them by their basic patterns. In our lessons we will examine the two basic patterns and some variations. One pattern is usually called psalms of descriptive praise. We refer to these as the psalms of joy in our lessons. Another pattern is the psalms of lament. For the purpose of our study, let's call these the psalms of pain. The names we use are not nearly as important as the ideas of the patterns themselves.

Authorship of the Psalms

David is the central figure in the psalms, but he is not the writer of the entire collection, as is sometimes supposed. The superscriptions that appear before the first verse in many translations of the psalms often give notice as to the presumed author. Seventy-three of the psalms are attributed to David in these superscriptions—the text above the main part of the psalm that gives information about the author and the events or situation from which the psalm was written. But other psalms are attributed to a variety of other writers, including Moses (Psalm 90), Solomon (Psalms 72, 132), Heman (Psalm 88), Ethan (Psalm 89), Asaph (for example, Psalm 50), and the guild of composers descended from Korah (such as Psalm 42). Many psalms are anonymous (such as Psalms 145–150).

The question of the authorship of the psalms is complex, and the subject of the collection and arrangement of the psalms is even more complex. They were written over a period of a thousand years. From the time of Moses to the time of Ezra, psalms of worship were being written by men and women, including priests and laypeople and kings and prophets.

God in the Psalms

Last, we must observe the importance of the person of God in the psalms, for they are addressed to Him; they are also the responses of His people to Him. The psalms present the praises of God's people, they elevate His name, and they make glorious His person. They also present the complaints of God's people for the troubles they encounter in their daily living.

But the psalms center on God. To read them merely to describe human emotions, to rhapsodize over the beauty of nature, or to share an aesthetic experience in great literature is ultimately to misread the psalms. In them, we confront in ever new ways the person of Yahweh, God of Israel, God and Father of the Lord Jesus Christ.

While there are various ways to categorize the psalms for study purposes, for our journey in discovering psalms, we have divided them into eight divisions and have selected certain psalms to be representative of each division for our discussion. The eight divisions are as follows:

Psalms of worship: 15, 29, 48, 54, 57, 61, 84, 87, 95, 100, 108, 117, 134, 135, 136, 148.

Psalms of joy: 30, 33, 34, 63, 66, 67, 68, 75, 76, 81, 92, 96, 105, 108, 113, 114, 115, 116, 122, 124, 126, 133, 138, 145, 146, 147, 148, 150.

Psalms of pain: 3, 4, 5, 6, 7, 9, 10, 12, 13, 17, 20, 28, 31, 35, 38, 39, 40, 41, 44, 51, 54, 55, 56, 57, 59, 60, 64, 69, 70, 71, 74, 77, 79, 80, 83, 85, 86, 88, 94, 101, 102, 109, 120, 123, 130, 137, 140, 141, 142, 143, 144.

Psalms of the wise: 1, 8, 14, 36, 37, 49, 50, 52, 53, 58, 78, 82, 90, 103, 106, 107, 111, 112, 119, 127, 128, 139.

Psalms of trust: 11, 18, 23, 25, 27, 31, 32, 42, 43, 46, 61, 62, 73, 91, 121, 125, 129, 131.

Psalms of nature: 19, 65, 104, 148.

Psalms of the King: 2, 21, 24, 45, 47, 72, 89, 93, 98, 99, 132.

Psalms of the Savior: 16, 22, 97, 110, 118.

There is one further category not included in our study, the psalms of ascent, which were used for the pilgrims on their way to Jerusalem.

Together, let's begin to discover the book of Psalms.

Psalms of Worship

◆———————◆

Lord, You are good; Your mercy is everlasting;
Your truth endures to all generations. Amen.

Where to Begin?

Perhaps the hardest thing we face as we open the book of
Psalms is knowing where to begin. With most books we
would simply open to the beginning and then read through
to the end. We can read the psalms this way, of course, and
many do just that. Indeed, there are some Bible readers who
read through the book of Psalms each month. They read five
psalms and one chapter of Proverbs each day of the month.
But for those just starting out, the book is so large that this
reading pattern would likely be intimidating.

The book of Psalms, however, does have a beginning and
an ending. Psalm 1 sets the stage of reverence and contemplation. Psalm 150 is an uproarious conclusion, like an organ
played with all the stops out. But the distance between the
first and last psalm is so extensive that it would be easy for us
to lose our way without some guidance.

Open and Read?

Another way to approach the book of Psalms is to just open
the book at random and read whatever strikes our fancy at

the moment. Since the poems are independent units, there is really nothing wrong with this approach because the book of Psalms is a loose collection of 150 different units.

Reading with a Plan

Perhaps a better approach is to come to the book of Psalms with a plan that is based on thematic ideas and distinct forms of poetry. By learning about these several types of psalms, we are then able to explore other psalms of similar types with some degree of familiarity. This is the way we shall study the psalms in these lessons.

In our study we shall view the psalms in eight broad categories. These categories are based on two concepts—the literary form and thematic issues or topics.

These categories are not mutually exclusive, as some psalms might fit into more than one grouping. An unusual number of psalms will fit into a few categories, while some other categories include fewer psalms. But having an awareness of these categories will help us in our study.

All Psalms Are Worship Psalms

This title for our first category and lesson is "Psalms of Worship." Actually, *all* the psalms are psalms of worship. They were all meant to be sung in the public, community worship of God in the Temple in Jerusalem in biblical times. More than anything else, the psalms focus on the person of God and how His people may come to Him in delightful response, somber reflection, awestruck wonder, collective song, and even clapping and dance. However, we will select several psalms at the beginning of our study that focus on the worship of God in a particular way.

Special Psalms of Worship

The psalms focus on worship in a variety of ways, but in this lesson we shall examine several psalms that center particularly on the worship of God. These are selected on the basis of their contributions to our understanding of the topic and also with regard to the variety of expression they present.

In this lesson we shall look closely at Psalm 100.

Psalm 100—Enter Joyfully

A Mood Set to Music

Psalm 100 is a mood set to music—the mood of joy in the shape of a psalm of praise. Here is a splendid place to begin our study of the psalms. For here we discover that the psalms do not simply convey information; they set moods and express emotions. They are poetry, and as in all poetry, the experience the poem presents is paramount. In Psalm 100, that experience is pure joy.

Psalm 100 may be one of the most familiar of the psalms of worship, as it is used in many churches as an opening call to worship. Perhaps the most arresting quality about the wording of this psalm is its emphasis on joy and delight. It has an exuberance that is nearly childlike. As children rush to the Christmas tree early Christmas morning, so, too, the worshippers in biblical times thronged with joyful abandon to the Temple in Jerusalem for the worship of God. The opening words reflect this mood: "Make a joyful noise to the LORD, all the earth! Serve the LORD with gladness! Come into his presence with singing!" (100:1–2, ESV).

A Worship in Sadness

When some people think of worship in biblical times, they tend to think nearly exclusively of blood and guilt and of sin and death. The reasons for these thoughts are clear. So much of the biblical guidelines on worship in ancient Israel center on animal sacrifice as God's method for bringing deliverance from sin and guilt that we get the idea that all worship in biblical times was somber and melancholy—composed primarily of weeping, contrition, and fasting.

A Worship in Delight

But not all worship of God was sad. In fact, worship could also be centered in laughter, joy, and dance. Along with the times of contemplation and confession, there were also times of celebrative joy, of great feasting, of spiritual "partying" in the presence of the Lord.

Psalm 100, written to be sung, presents this joyful attitude. Its message is that the people should come to the Temple in a spirit of celebration.

God Is So Good

Psalm 100 gives us one of the central teachings of the psalms, an underlying motivation for the worship of God. This basic idea may sound trite, but it is profound, "For the LORD is good; His mercy and lovingkindness are everlasting, His faithfulness [endures] to all generations" (100:5, AMP).

There is a profound nobility and grandeur to these words that send a chill up and down one's spine. We have heard them before and are accustomed to them. But their familiarity doesn't diminish their eternal truth—our God is good!

Some "Gods" Are Not So Good

A Christian couple spent some time in Taiwan, and on their free days, they would visit sites around the city, including some of shrines to local gods. They were fascinated by the concept that a belief in so many deities meant that there were good gods and evil gods. To complicate matters, the good gods weren't always completely good and the gods who were evil were often profoundly bad.

In the Tao shrines of the Taiwanese, there were so many gods and goddesses that the couple found it impossible to keep track of them all, but the basic idea involved the searching for balance between deities who were capricious and destructive and those who were more benign. They also learned that certain days were somehow better for some gods, and certain locations were more ideal for making contact with other gods. They learned that people sometimes traveled a long way to get to just the right place to make contact with a good god, but there was never any assurance of the god's response. To this Christian couple, this system of worship seemed to be kind of a game of chance, a gambling with deities.

Concepts like this were common in the world of the Old Testament.

Baal and Asherah

Only when a person grasps the notion of good and gods do the words of the psalms take on their original, authentic excitement. In biblical times, Israel was surrounded by pagan people who had belief systems controlled by gods who were not good. One of these gods was Baal. Another was the goddess Asherah. Baal and Asherah were fertility deities in the worship symbols of the people of Canaan.

Baal was particularly associated with storms and crops; Asherah was associated with fertility and various war symbols. These and many other gods were crazed by sexual drives and blood lust. They were petty and unpredictable, yet at times noble and dignified. They incited the basest instincts in people, preyed on their fears, and jostled for power with one another. Petty and unpredictable gods like these were no good.

What If God Were Not Good?

Now, just suppose there was one god, and he was like one of the pagan gods of the ancient Near East. This would be the worst imaginable situation. For there to be one god who was like Baal or one goddess who was like Asherah would be hell on earth. Imagine, if you can, one god or goddess in charge of the world who was against you, who wasn't good, but was selfish and evil. A god who acted on caprice, not principle, who was capable of bribery and deceit.

Israel's Glory: God Is Good!

But Israel's great distinction from all the surrounding pagan nations was that the one true God had revealed Himself to His people as unique and altogether good. The idea of God's goodness was not an evolutionary progress of thought, nor a bold, daring risk of faith on the part of the people of Israel. Rather, God's goodness was His own statement, His own revelation about Himself.

This is one of the most exciting and comforting of all biblical truths. There is one true God, and we don't need to play the games the ancients had to play in pitting one god against another. Furthermore, we have assurance that the one completely good God is *for* us, not *against* us. And we know that He wills good for us and that He speaks and acts in truth.

So, Come with Joy!

For us today, the lesson is the same as it was to people more than 2,500 years ago. Since God is good and His mercy is everlasting, we may come to worship Him in joy and not in terror. We don't need to be afraid of God. Everyone who knows God through Jesus Christ may approach Him boldly, confidently in worship: "Let us therefore come boldly unto the throne of grace, that we may obtain mercy, and find grace to help in time of need" (Hebrews 4:16, KJV).

To worship God is to respond to His goodness with joy and delight. Here is one of the central biblical teachings on worship; it is the message of Psalm 100.

Psalm 95—Enter Reverently

Psalm 95 is another of the psalms of worship that helps to set a balance with the mood of Psalm 100. This psalm begins in much the same manner as Psalm 100, with a delighted and joyful call to the people to worship God as a community, using plural pronouns: "Oh come, let *us* sing to the LORD; let *us* make a joyful noise to the rock of *our* salvation! Let *us* come into his presence with thanksgiving; let *us* make a joyful noise to him with songs of praise! For the LORD is a great God, and a great King above all gods" (95:1–3, ESV; italics added for emphasis).

Come Together to Worship God

Sometimes we tend to think of the worship of God in very personal terms. We may focus on private responses and inward attitudes in quiet moments. This is why some people say they can worship God quite well beside a stream or in solitude. The Bible does not ignore these ideas, but neither does it concentrate on them.

When the Bible speaks of worship, the emphasis is the actions and attitudes we share together as God's people. The psalms of worship have phrases such as, "Let us sing!" "Let us make a joyful noise." "Let us come before his presence." Worship is what we do together, for we cannot be fully Christian in isolation. This is the reason the writer of the book of Hebrews emphasizes the importance of our meeting together for worship: "Let us draw near to God with a sincere heart . . . Let us hold unswervingly to the hope we profess . . . let us consider how we may spur one another on toward love and good deeds, not giving up meeting together" (Hebrews 10:22–25, NIV).

God Is So Great!

The exuberant, joyful praise of God with which Psalm 95 begins centers on His greatness, His rule, and His creative actions. From time to time, as you will see in Psalm 95:3, the writers of these songs will speak of God in relationship to the gods of Israel's neighbor nations. When the Psalmists say that the Lord is a King above all gods, this is not that they give credibility to other deities. Rather, this is just another way in which the poets express their awesome reverence for the Lord. For purposes of argument, they momentarily grant the idea of other gods, then debase them before the surpassing greatness of the Lord. It is as though the Psalmists are saying, "Do you believe in other gods? The Lord is King over all supposed deities."

Whereas Psalm 100 celebrates the goodness of God, Psalm 95 focuses on His greatness, and in speaking of God's greatness, we mean several things. His greatness speaks of His majesty, His power, and His sovereignty. The shout "God is great!" is an affirmation that there is no one greater. All power is His, all rule is His, all glory is His. He is King of all! The Lord is great! We who live many centuries after this psalm was written can scarcely be less impressed with the idea of God's greatness than those who first sang these words and shouted the affirmation.

Worship in Quiet Wonder

The second movement of Psalm 95 begins at verse 6, "Oh come, let *us* worship and bow down; let *us* kneel before the Lord, *our* Maker!" (ESV; italics added). This is a dramatic change of mood from the first verses. The focus on the psalm is now on reverent adoration, collective contemplation, and a trusting submission to His wonder. Here we sense something of the profound idea that He is God! And as God, He desires our worship.

As we read these words, we share with the writer the profound swell of wonder, of awe and reverence, of the God we come together to worship. As "sophisticated" Christians living in the twenty-first century, who live in a complex high-tech world, it is easy to lose much of the sense of wonder that pervades the Bible. But as we kneel before the One who created all that we see, feel, and enjoy, we, too, are overwhelmed by His greatness!

Let Us Kneel

The verbs in verse 6 are all words describing physical posture. The term translated "worship" is the Hebrew word meaning "to prostrate oneself." And the verb is buttressed by words meaning to bow down and to kneel. The idea here gives us another model for the worship of God—quiet submission and reverent adoration.

Kneeling is a physical posture used to express the inner feelings of the worshipper. It is very natural in scriptural worship for a person who feels a sense of submission and gratitude to God to *bow down*, to *kneel*, to prostrate oneself. Then, too, it is appropriate to express joy and delight in our worship of God.

Worship in Obedience

Yet another aspect of worship emerges in the third movement of Psalm 95. This begins in the last line of verse 7 with the words, "Today, if you will hear His voice" (NASB). This new factor is obedience.

In this movement of Psalm 95 we learn that worship is not only singing and laughing, nor is it accomplished simply by posture or the position of our bodies. All of these are important to worship, but none is the whole of it. Finally, ultimately, there must be obedience.

Obedience Is Better Than Sacrifice

The words "to obey is better than sacrifice" (1 Samuel 15:22, KJV) can be rephrased on the basis of Psalm 95. There is no genuine worship apart from obedience to God. Psalm 95 begins with shouting, singing, and rejoicing. It then speaks of the hushed contemplation of worshippers who are physically prone before the majesty of their great God. And it ends with a command to obey God and gives a warning based on the experiences of the people of Israel in the wilderness when they disobeyed God (95:10). Worship without obedience is meaningless.

Warnings from the Wilderness

You recall the Exodus and the wilderness experience of the Israelites and their failure to obey God. A whole generation who participated in that rebellion were not permitted to cross the Jordan and enter the Promised Land. It is not unusual for the psalm writers to include references to the historical experiences of Israel, for those experiences were designed to teach successive generations lessons of obedience to the Lord.

The King James Version uses the words "provocation" and "temptation" in verse 8: "Harden not your heart, as in *the provocation*, and as in *the day of temptation* in the wilderness" (italics added), revealing a subtle play on words that is otherwise lost in our English translations. The original Hebrew words for those terms became place names in Israel's experience in the wilderness (see Exodus 17:7 and Numbers 20:13), which are mentioned in more recent translations. The Amplified Version translates verse 8 this way: "Do not harden your hearts and become spiritually dull as at *Meribah* [the place of strife], and as at *Massah* [the place of testing] in the wilderness" (italics added). These rebellions and their consequences stand as perpetual reminders to people of faith of the folly of disobedience. Obedience is not only a part of worship; ultimately, it is what validates the whole worship experience.

Going through the Motions

These psalms that are so old still speak to us today. It is still possible for people to go through all the right motions in public worship, but unless their day-to-day actions are directed by the word of the Lord in obedience to His purposes, their worship is hollow. Obedience in worship is not just one thing; it becomes the only thing.

Psalm 48—O Jerusalem!

Jerusalem—Not Just the City

When we listen to or watch the news, we often hear phrases like these: "Washington today declared . . ." or "The meeting between Moscow and Beijing took place . . ." We know that the newscaster or writer is not talking only about those cities or their populations; they are using those city names as stand-ins, a shorthand or symbol for the entire country of which the cities are the capitals.

The psalm writers used Jerusalem in a similar way. Jerusalem in biblical times was the place of the Temple. Jerusalem was where God made Himself known to His people. And for the people of Israel, the Temple was the center of worship, so much so that Exodus and Deuteronomy commanded all Hebrew men to make three pilgrimages to Jerusalem each year. It was there, too, the people offered their sacrifices to God in worship.

This is why the psalm writers will mention Jerusalem as a sort of shorthand to mean the meeting place between God and His people. In Psalms, Jerusalem represents God and humankind coming together through worship. And the opposite is true also. When Psalms 100 and 95 call for joyful procession in the worship of God, the place they intend for us to think about is Jerusalem.

Jerusalem—God's Gift

Psalm 48 is a song of praise to the Lord for His gift of Jerusalem as the center of worship. As you read this psalm, attempt to discover deep in your being something of the joy the poet feels for this beautiful old city.

The Place for Worship

The first movement of the psalm (verses 1–3) offers praise to God that Jerusalem—"the city of our God" (translated this way in virtually all English translations)—is indeed the center of worship. Since the Temple was situated at the city's highest point, it was inconceivable for the writer to think of true worship of God being conducted in any other place. While Jerusalem was a much loved place for all Jews, the praise for the city expressed in this psalm is related entirely to its being the center for worship—"the city of our God! His holy mountain" (48:1, ESV).

The Response of Kings

The second movement of the psalm (verses 4–8) is more difficult to understand. Since verses 4–7 speak of kings recoiling in horror or moving away in trembling wonder from the city of Jerusalem, we can reasonably ask when such events ever happened in biblical history. Our search for references will lead us to conclude that these verses do not describe historical events.

Such being the case, we are left with several possibilities. One is to say that the words are rhetorical in nature, glorifying the city by elaborate images. This is certainly possible, as the poets of the Bible often use lavish language for effect.

A Future Day

But here is another possibility, one that might take us closer
to the truth. That is to think of these verses from a prophetic
perspective—a future time when all of earth's rulers will
marvel at what the Lord has done in Jerusalem. This idea
seems reasonable to consider because of the pattern in the
psalms that looks to a future time when the world's leaders will recognize the rule of God as King in His holy city,
Jerusalem (see Psalms 2:10; 138:4).

Jerusalem—The Everlasting City

Verse 8 seems to stress the feeling of confidence that God will
ultimately establish Jerusalem, "the city of the LORD Almighty,
in the city of our God" (NIV), as the center of worship for all
eternity.

The City of the Savior

As Christians, at least two responses to this ancient hymn are
open to us. One is to take a bold look back to the death and
Resurrection of Jesus. These events took place in Jerusalem,
and they gave meaning to all the worship that had transpired
in the Temple in biblical times. In this way, the presence of
the city of Jerusalem in the story of our salvation is assured.
If nothing else of significance ever happened in Jerusalem,
the events associated with the death and Resurrection of Jesus
would ensure the importance of the city in Christian thought
and imagination forever.

The City of God's Future Rule

But there is the possibility that the words of Psalm 48:8 extend into the future. If so, the reference may be to the idea held by many Christians that God will in some way at some future time establish His Kingdom on earth with Jerusalem as the capital.

If you have ever been to Jerusalem, you might have felt what some visitors have described about their time there—a sense of what should be against what one finds. We look forward to a day when Jerusalem will once more be the center of the rule of God. The psalms and the prophets speak of this hope often (Psalms 2, 110; Zephaniah 3:14–18). The writers of the New Testament look forward as well to the New Jerusalem (Revelation 21:10).

Jerusalem is the site of the biblical Temple. It is the place of the death and Resurrection of Jesus Christ. It may well also be a model of the New Jerusalem. No wonder the Psalmists called it "the city of our God."

Jerusalem and God's Lovingkindness

The third movement of Psalm 48 (verses 9–14) returns to the subject of the praise of God. The centerpiece of the poem is verse 9: "Within your temple, O God, we meditate on your unfailing love" (NIV). The Hebrew word translated "unfailing love" is one of the most important words in the psalms to describe the person of God. Other versions translate it as "lovingkindness," "goodness," "steadfast love," "gracious love," "constant love," "faithful love," "mercy," or "loving devotion."

No single English word can capture the essence of the Hebrew word, but each of these translation choices suggests one facet of God's love, and together we see a picture of His

care as eternal, enduring, faithful, constant, kind, merciful—
loving and loyal.

A Loving Look

These closing verses of Psalm 48 describe in an almost sensual
manner the attitude of the people toward Jerusalem. As lovers
might explore each other's bodies, so the lovers of Jerusalem
explore its beauties, caress its stones, and learn its features.
And in the city, there is the way to God. In a tone of awe, the
Psalmist writes, "For such is God, our God forever and ever;
He will lead us until death" (48:14, NASB).

So God and the city are tied together in this psalm of worship because of the true worship of the Lord.

Our Jerusalems

To reflect on this psalm is to get a renewed appreciation of
the freedom we have to worship God in the places and in the
manner of our own choosing. In Old Testament times, there
was only one center of worship and that was Jerusalem. Today,
with churches on several corners in a community, we have
freedom of choice never imagined in biblical times. There is a
sense in which we each have our "Jerusalem," the place where
we come together to worship the Lord.

Psalm 54—Sacrifice Freely

A Rediscovery of Deliverance

Psalm 54 is one of the psalms of pain, a category we explore
in lesson 3. But we'll include it here because of its remarkable

conclusion in verses 6–7. Here David has rediscovered the help of God and His gracious deliverance from an experience of terror as he was about to be destroyed by a military force sent by King Saul. Out of this experience David comes to the worship of God with joyful abandon as he says, "Willingly I will sacrifice to You; I will praise Your name, LORD, for it is good" (54:6, NASB).

Here is a poem of personal experience as David speaks from his heart. His experience of rediscovering the presence of God in his life causes him to renew his desire to worship Him, to bring sacrifices of joy, to make much of God's name, to exult in His goodness.

A Motivation for Worship

These words in verse 6 are significant because they indicate the kind of obedience that is called for in the psalms for the worship of God. And in Psalm 54 we have the personal testimony of one who is obeying the command to worship God with his whole being.

David had experienced deliverance from death, and he didn't need to be told to worship God; he wanted to with all his heart.

Commands and Experience

It is here in the psalms that the commands to worship God and our own experiences of His goodness come together. God who reaches into our lives with His goodness also commands that we worship Him. When we have experienced His goodness, we respond immediately in joyous worship. Worship is harder when we feel that God is distant. This is what leads to the psalms of pain in lesson 3. But for now, think back across the years to those special high moments when you felt close to God. Then combine those experiences with the urgings and commands that come from Him, and you will find renewed motivation for the true worship of God.

The fact that God gives so many commands to worship Him suggests how prone we are to neglect this important act. When we hear the command from Him and already have reasons within us, then, as it was with David, we are likely to worship freely, with integrity and joy.

Psalm 57—Singing before the Dawn

To Awaken the Dawn

For our purposes in this lesson, read verses 7–11 of this psalm, where the Psalmist vows to praise God in the community worship services. Here he is so overcome with the renewed sense of the presence of God in his life that he promises his praises will awaken the very dawn. As the crowing of a rooster is a response to the dawn, the Psalmist audaciously says the dawn will come in response to his singing. This figurative use of language is for effect, of course. He means that he will already be singing before the first rays of the sun streak across the eastern sky. Here is an enthusiasm for the worship of God that cannot be contained. As we read and reread these five short verses that explode with praise, we can't help but join with the Psalmist when he says, "Be exalted, O God, above the heavens! Let your glory be over all the earth!" (57:11, ESV).

Psalm 61—Daily Vows

The Sacrifices of Praise

Again, for this lesson, we may read the last verse of this psalm of trust in God for another glimpse at the subject of worship. The Psalmist says he is determined to live his life in the praise of God. Daily, he says, he will fulfill his vows.

The specific vows this verse suggests are those of praise. We will discover more about this in lesson 3 on the psalms of pain. But the basic idea is that when we pray to God for deliverance, implicit in that prayer is the vow that when God has acted in mercy, we will tell others about it and in doing so will praise the Lord's name.

We find this idea expressed so clearly by the writer of the book of Hebrews: "Through Jesus, therefore, let us continually offer to God a sacrifice of praise—the fruit of lips that openly profess his name. And do not forget to do good and to share with others, for with such sacrifices God is pleased" (Hebrews 13:15–16, NIV). The spirit and the sound of these words of the Hebrews writer are much the same as the words of the Psalmist: "Then I will ever sing in praise of your name and fulfill my vows day after day" (61:8, NIV). Believers since the beginning of time who experience the saving actions of God naturally desire to express their love for God, their gratitude for His mercy, and for His unending love. This is the vow of praise, which is an essential part of the worship of God.

Psalm 29—Majestic Praise

They All Say, "Glory!"

There is a special mystique to this psalm. Its language is based in part upon associations with the poetry of the Canaanite people who preceded Israel in the land. For our purposes in this lesson, however, we can read it as an exuberant psalm of the worship of God. Notice especially the opening and closing verses. The psalm begins with a call to worship God in the beauty of holiness (29:2), and it concludes with the shouts of all the people for His great glory (29:9). The God whose thunder majestically dulls the noise of the ocean waves, whose shattering voice sets the trees to dancing and causes deer to give birth to their fawns—this God speaks in peace to His people! The stability of His power and the strength of His reign encourage those who trust in Him.

So they come to worship Him!

And so we may come!

In Summary

When we turn our Bibles to the book of Psalms, we open it to a book of worship. We can scarcely think of the psalms properly without being driven to consider, to study, to understand, and—most importantly—to participate in the worship of God. Whether it is in the quiet and contemplative words of Psalm 95 or the bombastic thunder of Psalm 29, the psalms all press us hard to worship. They urge, compel, exemplify, and exude the varied attitudes, moods, and approaches of the true worship of God.

As we read and reflect on these ancient words, we can seek to apply them in our own lives. This will primarily be in terms of our attitudes and our motivation in worship. True worship is not nearly so much a matter of form as it is of inward expression. Biblical worship in the Temple is a world away from our worship patterns in the twenty-first-century church. But the underlying issues remain the same. God still seeks true worshippers (John 4:23). And there is no better place to begin to think about worship than in the psalms.

Truly to contemplate the importance of the psalms in worship is to imagine the unthinkable: what would biblical worship be if there were no psalms?

◆————————————————◆

Lord, You are mighty. You are full of glory and strength.
I worship You in the beauty of holiness. AMEN.

PSALM 29

The voice of the Lord is over the waters; the God of glory thunders, the Lord thunders over the mighty waters.

—Psalm 29:3, NIV

God speaks to us in many different ways. Within the Scriptures we find a range of parables, instructions, laments, encouragements, rebukes, and promises. God communicates with us in various ways so that each individual can find a way to hear Him.

In Psalm 29, our Lord's voice is depicted as booming and powerful. Yet He spoke to Elijah in a still, small voice (1 Kings 19:12).

This week I found myself praying, "Lord, why can't You be louder? I need direction and I'm not hearing You. A booming megaphone voice from the sky would be lovely." As I prayed, I realized that God has plenty to share with me. My problem is that I don't open my heart to listen to all the ways in which He might choose to speak.

The voice of loud thunderstorms can remind me of His creative power and strength—strength I need to face the challenges of the day. Other times I hear Him during a tender conversation with a friend—His compassion whispering to my heart. When I seek Him in the Bible, His Spirit brings new life to familiar words. The rustle of dry leaves speaks of death and new life. The warble of bird-song reassures me that He knows each sparrow. A piercing siren in the distance declares that we live in a world of suffering, and He calls me to serve the hurting. The range of instruments in a praise band shows me how each unique person brings a valuable sound to the whole.

Instead of complaining to God that He isn't speaking to me, I asked Him to open my ears to hear.

—*Sharon Hinck*

Notes

Notes

Psalms of Joy

*Lord, I rejoice in You and praise You; I sing unto
You a new song because Your Word is right and
Your works are true. AMEN.*

Feelings

Feelings and emotions are fundamental expressions of our
basic humanity—the essential aspects of our being truly
human. Each of us may feel things and express those feelings
in different ways, but it is an undeniable fact that as people—
God's special creation—feelings are very much a part of us
and are important to us.

We do not always come to the Bible with a balanced view
of what it has to say about our humanity. Sometimes when we
reflect on the message of the Bible, we think merely in terms
of what it has to say about truth and behavior. In other words,
we may read the Bible to discover what to believe and how to
act. But these appeals to the intellect and to the will are not
the complete message of the Bible. There is something more.

We may also read the Bible to learn about our feelings. And
nowhere in the Bible are feelings more present and predomi-
nant than in the book of Psalms. The psalms focus on our
feelings; this is their strong suit.

The Pursuit of Pleasure

Among the varied feelings the writers of the psalms express is
the emotion of joy, the sense of delight. Rightly so! After all,
we all want to be happy; each of us wishes to experience joy
in life. The Declaration of Independence leads us to believe
that the pursuit of happiness is one of our unalienable rights
endowed by our Creator.

For some people, though, the pursuit of happiness degen-
erates into shallowness and silliness. We might spend hours
shopping on the Internet or watching shopping channels,
hopeful that one frivolous purchase delivered to our front
door will help fill whatever emptiness we feel inside. We glue
our thumbs and our eyes to the screens of our smartphones,
hoping our electronic communications might fill the loneli-
ness within.

Or maybe our pursuit of happiness becomes a life devoted
entirely to the pursuit of happiness. Addictions, compulsive
behavior, abuse of others or our environment, materialism,
hedonism, and selfishness are some of the distortions of the
chase after pleasure.

For the Psalmists, the route to happiness is quite different.
For them, the true pursuit of happiness is found only in an
abiding relationship with God in association with others of
like spirit. These Psalmists tell us that a deep and rich joy may
be found in the Lord and in our relationship to Him. They
also speak of the joy to be found in the community of people
that shares faith in God. This means that one of the significant elements in the book of Psalms are those songs we term

the psalms of joy. Among these are Psalms 33, 66, 67, 75, 96, and 150.

Psalm 33—Rejoice in the Lord

A Call to Joy

The opening verses of Psalm 33 set the stage for our understanding of the psalms of joy. The psalm begins with a call for God's people to gather together in joyful praise of the Lord: "Sing for joy in the LORD, you righteous ones; praise is becoming to the upright. Give thanks to the LORD with the lyre; sing praises to Him with a harp of ten strings. Sing to Him a new song; play skillfully with a shout of joy" (verses 1–3, NASB).

These beautiful poetic words proclaim the truth that the praise of God is a happy task. By rejoicing in Him, we experience a profound sense of inner joy and happiness. Praise is a spiritual tonic. When we praise the Lord, we find our own spirits lifted, our outlook brightened, and our life takes on a whole new meaning.

These psalms of joy have a rather simple pattern. First, there is the call for people to praise God, and second, we are given the reasons for praising God.

Verses 1–3 give us the call to praise God; the heart of the psalm—verses 4–19—gives many reasons to praise Him. Then follows a concluding section (verses 20–22), which is a prayer of dependent hope.

It will likely be helpful to reduce this pattern to an outline:
- A call to praise God in joyful praise and music (verses 1–3)

- Reasons for the praise of God (verses 4–19)
- His work in creation (verses 4–9)
- His work among the nations of the world (verses 10–15)
- His work in His people (verses 16–19)
- A prayer of dependent hope in God (verses 20–22)

The particular call to praise in verses 1–3 uses a series of imperatives: rejoice, praise, sing, play skillfully. These words are plural commands that are addressed to the people. We find a recurring pattern in the psalms in which the people of God are commanded to respond to Him in exuberant worship. But these are always set in a framework of joy. Praise is pleasant, even beautiful. It is pleasant for those who participate, and it brings pleasure and joy to God.

Praise in Music

A second reading of these opening verses reveals a focus on music in the praise of God. The Psalmist calls for singing and playing, for skill and involvement, and throughout the psalm an emphasis is placed on the balance of art and heart in worship. And balance in worshipful music is difficult to achieve.

Churches today can still be battlegrounds on which "worship wars" are fought. In an effort to please everyone in the congregation, churches might divide their Sunday morning service in two: an early traditional service with pipe organ and piano playing hymns, and a later contemporary service with guitars, drums, and synthesizers playing new praise songs and choruses.

Throughout the history of the church there have been countless battles over styles or types of music used in the worship of God. Yet a principle easily demonstrated from that same history is that music lives as music progresses. Whenever there is an attempt to freeze musical style in the expressions of a particular period, music begins to lose its power to communicate a worshipful experience among believers in response to God. Yet in time, one period's limitation becomes the next era's standard.

The Psalmist's instructions to "sing unto him a new song" (33:3, KJV) not only call for new music but also demand that all music used in the worship of God be sung with a new heart of genuine response to God.

Some of the Reasons

It is appropriate to ask ourselves why it is important to sing a new joyful song to the accompaniment of musical instruments in our praise of God. The psalms give us two reasons. First, we praise Him because of who He is. Second, we praise Him because of what He does.

As we come to the second movement of Psalm 33 (verses 4–9), we find a focus on God's creative actions. These are marvelous creation themes in which God's mighty acts found in Genesis 1 are framed in poetry and set to music. And as we remember, one of the great teachings in the Creation story is that what God made was "very good" (Genesis 1, ESV)—all of creation is an expression of His excellence.

The next stanza of Psalm 33 (verses 10–15) speaks of God's work among the people and nations of the world. First, God is to be praised for His love and care for all people everywhere.

Second, God is to be praised because of His wisdom: "But the plans of the Lord stand firm forever" (33:11, NIV). No human plans can negate or take from God's plans, and no human endeavor is eternal, as God's are. Then comes the awesome promise: "Blessed is the nation whose God is the Lord" (verse 12, NIV). Yes, God cared for His special people, the Israelites, but He is also working in the lives of all people everywhere.

The Eyes of the Lord

The next section of Psalm 33 is made up of verses 16–19. The references here are to God's dealings with people of faith. When our heart and attitude are right with God, we will have a healthy attitude toward ourselves. With colorful picture language, the Psalmist makes the point that only God is worthy of our trust—in Him there is final victory. To put our trust in anything else—massive armies, mighty war horses—is "a vain thing." Our trust and hope are only in God.

Verse 18 has an electric message for us: "Behold, the eye of the Lord is on those who fear him, on those who hope in his steadfast love" (ESV).

We know that the "eye of the Lord" is on everybody in a general sense (see verse 13). But there is something special about the Lord's care for those who are faithful to Him.

The phrase "those who fear him" does not imply that we are to be afraid of God. The Hebrew verb "to fear" when used in this context speaks of reverent adoration, faithful response, and a readiness to worship and serve him. To "fear the Lord" is a biblical way to describe saving faith and abiding trust.

And So We Wait

The concluding verses of Psalm 33 (20–22) take on the form of a prayer of response, a declaration of dependent trust. Because the believer knows that the eyes of the Lord are directed toward him, he or she is content to wait on Him for final deliverance (verse 20). But our waiting is not passive; it is not a time of inactivity. The Hebrew verb translated "to wait" is active. It is not a slumping in a hammock awaiting the evening breeze; to wait on the Lord is to continue to live in active trust in His mercy. We are to be busy in our Master's business. It was Jesus Himself who told us to, as the English Standard Version translates it, "Engage in business [use the gifts God has entrusted us with] until I come" (Luke 19:13).

Verse 21 of the psalm is significant as the Psalmist writes, "For our heart shall rejoice in him" (KJV). The word "rejoice" in verse 1 is in the imperative—a command. In verse 21, "rejoice" is in the indicative—a statement of fact. First came the command, and then followed the obedient response. In this, the Psalmist has given us our model. As Christians, we are to be people who are so full of joy and happiness that everyone around us can see it. Why? Because of our relationship with God, who is our joy!

Psalm 66—Make a Joyful Noise

Joy and Song

For many readers of the psalms who don't sing well, the words "make a joyful noise unto God" are a comfort. But the

Hebrew word translated "noise" here actually means "to shout aloud." This is a term of explosive exuberance that marks the great joy of a person who loves the Lord and who is eager to express that love in an outward manner that others can see and hear.

While the words that open Psalm 66 seem to reflect a sense of abandon, the structure of the psalm is well-ordered. It is interesting to note that this contrast between what is said and the way in which it is said is a distinct feature of the psalms. This unusual feature may well be a model for the way we worship today—a combination of order and spontaneity, of planning and freedom.

Structure of a Psalm

Psalm 66 is more complex in organization and structure than Psalm 33, but there are several similarities in the broad design. Here is an outline of Psalm 66:

- An appeal for everybody—"all the earth"—to praise the Lord (verses 1–4)
- A report of the dramatic acts of the Lord that elicit praise (verses 5–7)
- A renewed appeal for people to praise the Lord in His protective care (verses 8–9)
- A report of the saving acts of the Lord that elicit praise (verses 10–12)
- A determination by the Psalmist that he will praise the Lord (verses 13–15)
- The confession of the Psalmist of the works of the Lord in his life (verses 16–20)

These six sections are an elaboration of the simpler three sections of Psalm 33. Remember that the basic pattern is made of a call to praise God, followed by a report of reasons to praise God. In Psalm 66 there is a call to praise Him, followed by reasons for that praise. Next there is a new call to praise Him and for new reasons. Then we have a personal statement by the Psalmist that he will praise God, and this is followed by a report of his praise.

It is important for us in our study to "feel" the flow of these psalms. Undoubtedly, most people may read through the psalm without ever thinking in terms of its structure—its outline and development. And it's unlikely that the ancient poets used an outline such as we have here, but they certainly wrote with a sense of movement and development. But as we twenty-first-century Christians try to understand what the ancient Hebrew writers were saying, our outline may help us grasp the meaning.

The Call for Joyful Praise

The writer's opening words in Psalm 66 tug forcefully at our emotions (verses 1–4). We catch the excitement of the Psalmist as he appeals to all the people of the earth to join together in one grand explosion of praise to the living God.

The troubling word translated as "terrible" in the King James Version (verses 3, 5) has been replaced in most modern translations as "awesome," another word whose meaning has shifted and diminished in recent decades. One version renders it as "fearsome." The Amplified Bible translates it as "awesome and fearfully glorious" in verse 3. The original

Hebrew word is related to the same word translated "to fear him" in Psalm 33:18, and here it means awe-inspiring, wonder-evoking.

What the Psalmist is doing here is praising God for His "awesome deeds for mankind" (verse 5, NIV).

To All the Nations

One of the remarkable features of the psalms is their inclusiveness. These were hymns used in the worship of the God of Israel in the Temple in Jerusalem. But contrary to the prevailing attitude of the people of Israel, the Psalmists did not restrict the praise of God to Hebrew people only. Over and over again there is the appeal to people of all nations—non-Jews—to join the people of Israel in praise to the Creator-God of heaven and earth. The universal thrust of the command in the first verse is matched by the prophecy of a coming time of worldwide praise to God in verse 4, "They will sing praises to Your name" (NASB). These words are a sharp reminder that God's plan from the beginning of His covenant with Abram (Abraham) was to include all people—to God there were no geographical or racial boundaries (Genesis 12:1–3). The grace of God flows out to everyone, including people whose culture and politics differ from ours.

Come and See

The appeal to "all the earth" in the first verse of the psalm is based upon the Old Testament ideal of missionary activity. For anyone who doubts that there was an outreach to others in ancient Israel, the words of this psalm certainly demonstrate that there was.

To the Christian, mission and evangelism are based on a concept of "go and tell," of following the "Great Commission" of Matthew 28:18–20. But in the earlier biblical period, the work of outreach—missionary activity—was stated differently. Psalm 66:5 explains it well: "Come and see what God has done" (ESV). The idea was that Israel was to live so close to the Lord, be so obedient to His word, and live such attractive and exemplary lives that neighboring nations would be impressed and would be drawn to them like iron filings to a magnet. In this way Israel's pagan neighbors would come to experience their God. They would "come and see" and would join in worship.

Our Soul among the Living

Renewed commands to offer praise to God appear in verses 8–9. In these verses there is an exquisitely tender line in the King James Version, describing God, who "holdeth our soul in life" (verse 9). The English Standard Version's wording says that God "has kept our soul among the living." What a wonderfully reassuring statement! God is the keeper and preserver of our lives. Life is His gift.

He Tests Our Mettle

Reasons for the praise of God take an unusual twist in verses 10–12. Here the Psalmist dares to jolt his listeners with the idea that God has tested His people in the past, even as a metallurgist might refine precious ore. The refining of silver is not intended to destroy it but to burn away anything that detracts from its value. It is by this refining process that the Lord brings out His purified people as a showcase of His handiwork.

I Will Fulfill My Vows

In the next to last section of Psalm 66 (verses 13–15), the Psalmist makes his vow of praise. His assertion is firm: "I will come to your temple with burnt offerings and fulfill my vows to you" (NIV).

Our modern world is vastly different from that of ancient Israel, and our patterns of worship have little resemblance to theirs. Their sacrifice of animals as "burnt offerings" seems abhorrent to us. Most of us feel squeamish over the idea of killing an animal for food. For those of us in urban and suburban environments, meat is something that comes in shrink-wrapped packaging in the meat cooler of a supermarket. And any thought of killing an animal as a sacrifice to God seems primitive and ludicrous.

The Very Best

In biblical times things were different. People in ancient Israel lived closer to nature. The breeding, birthing, and slaughter of animals was common to their way of life. But even then, according to their law, the offering of animals in sacrifice and worship was not only important; it was even a bit irrational.

Normally, an animal breeder will preserve the very best male for breeding purposes so as to improve the genetic quality of his herd. But the people of Israel had been told to go against this practice. They were to take the very best and offer it as the sacrificial offering to the Lord; they could do as they pleased with the rest of the herd. They had faith to believe that the quality of their herd was in the Lord's hands, and they were confident they would prosper by giving Him the best.

As Christians, we understand that every sacrifice of true worship in Old Testament times anticipated and foreshadowed the sacrificial death of Jesus—God's best for unworthy sinners. At the same time, it serves as a reminder for us to give of our best in worship and service to the Lord.

I Will Declare

Psalm 66 then concludes with the Psalmist's personal hymn of praise (verses 16–20). The act of worshipping God in the Temple period of the Old Testament involved far more than the offering of animal sacrifices. A profound part of their worship was the offering of words and songs of praise to their God. In these verses the Psalmist speaks of the richness of God's blessing as he offers praise. In this way, his words reinforce his actions of sacrificial worship. For the ancient Israelite, as for us today, his words in worship were important because they were expressions of the heart.

It is true, of course, that the paying of the vows of animal sacrifice referred to in our psalm (verses 13–15) is not a part of our worship today; however, the sacrifice of praise the Psalmist speaks of is very much a part of our relationship with God. We western Christians especially have become lax in our expressions of thanksgiving and praise to God, and because of this we have lost an exuberant richness from our spiritual lives. We would do well daily to echo the closing words of the psalm: "Praise be to God, who has not rejected my prayer or withheld his love from me!" (66:20, NIV).

Psalm 67—God Be Merciful

A Liturgy of Rejoicing

Psalm 67 is another type of psalm of joy. It is written as a brief liturgy, invoking the blessing of God on His people. The term *liturgy* is sometimes viewed in a disparaging manner as something done by rote—a lifeless ritual. In reality, there is no such thing as a dead liturgy, but there are some people who seem to be lifeless as they recite the liturgy. It is helpful to understand that the basic meaning of the term *liturgy* (derived from the Greek) is "the work of the people," an expression of public, communal worship.

The psalms give us our basis for liturgy in worship. Often, as in Psalm 67, there are "parts" to be sung or recited by different groups within the congregation. These are lines of response and counter-response, of bounding back and forth like a ping-pong ball across the table. This is another pattern of the psalms of joy.

His Face to Shine on Us

The opening verse of this psalm deserves special attention, as it illustrates an important feature of the psalms—the reworking of earlier Scripture in hymn settings. Our verse here reads,

"May God be gracious to us and bless us and make his face shine on us" (NIV).

These words are taken from the wonderful benediction that the Lord gave the priests of Israel for use in their worship together. It is usually called the Aaronic Benediction and is found in Numbers 6:24–26: "The LORD bless you and keep you; the LORD make his face shine on you and be gracious to you; the LORD turn his face toward you and give you peace" (NIV).

It is clear that Psalm 67:1 has taken the central verse of the Aaronic Benediction (Numbers 6:25) and has changed it only slightly in word order and in the pronouns. The verse in Numbers is spoken by the priest for the people; the verse in the psalm is spoken by the people on behalf of themselves.

The words "make his face to shine upon us" (67:1, ESV) speak of the light of God's presence. As Moses once experienced the light of the presence of God on his own face (Exodus 34:29), so the Psalmist asks for the light of the Lord's presence to be in their midst.

What a great line this is: God who is light making His face to shine on His people. This is a message of grace. It is a portrait of mercy. And it is also an anticipation of the life of the Lord Jesus.

A God with Skin On

"Daddy, what does God look like?" the boy asked his father. The boy's father told him that we can't see God, for He is Spirit. "But, Daddy," the little boy replied, "I want a God with skin on!" He wanted a tangible God he could see and feel.

In the person of the Lord Jesus, in His life and ministry, we have just what that little boy wanted—"a God with
skin on." Yes, Jesus was "a God with skin on" who attracted
people to Him by His winsome and loving manner. Again
and again we read that the people followed Him gladly. One
of the loveliest images from the Gospels is the picture of the
Lord Jesus surrounded by little children: "And he took them
up in his arms, put his hands upon them, and blessed them"
(Mark 10:16, KJV).

It is in the Savior Jesus that we have the fullest expression of
the anticipation of the Aaronic Benediction and the rephras-
ing of that blessing in the words of Psalm 67.

It is God's desire to bless His people. This was the intent
of the Lord in the original blessing. And this is echoed by
the writer of Psalm 67 as he closes with these words: "May
God bless us still, so that all the ends of the earth will fear
him" (NIV).

The blessing of God on His people, and the corresponding
response to Him of His people in fear—reverential awe—is
the suitable conclusion for a psalm of the liturgy of joy.

Psalm 75—We Give Thanks to You

The Nearness of His Name

There are psalms, as we will see in the next lesson, that speak
of God as distant and removed, seemingly unconcerned,
uncaring. But there are also psalms that exult in a sense of
His nearness—an exquisite reason to praise God. Psalm 75
begins this way. For the purposes of our lesson, we will only

look at the first verse of this psalm: "We give thanks to you, O God; we give thanks, for your name is near. We recount your wondrous deeds" (75:1, ESV).

The opening words, "We give thanks to you, O God," are prompted by a sense of God's presence. At times, this feeling comes in unexpected places and in unusual ways. We can be driving down a freeway, lost in thought, but suddenly feel the nearness of the Lord. Usually, though, the sense of the Lord's presence comes in times when we are worshipping together in church. This is certainly the idea expressed in the opening words of this psalm. Someone has wisely said that we can't be Christians in isolation. We experience God's nearness in our journey of faith as we meet together with our fellow Christians in worship.

Psalm 96—Sing a New Song

A Song among the Nations

This psalm begins with these majestic words: "Oh sing to the LORD a new song; sing to the LORD, all the earth!" (96:1, ESV). The idea of a "new song" first appeared in Psalm 33:3. Here in Psalm 96, though, the new song idea takes on an international dimension: "sing to the LORD, *all the earth*" (italics added). The praise of God that this psalm anticipates is multinational in nature. Verse 3 speaks of proclaiming God's glory among all the nations of the earth.

This is also a psalm that illuminates the truth that all creation joins in a grand chorus of praise. "Let the heavens rejoice, let the earth be glad; let the sea resound, and all that is in it. Let the fields be jubilant, and everything in them; let all the trees of the forest sing for joy" (verses 11–12, NIV). This sounds like nature's "Hallelujah" chorus!

If you have ever attended a missionary conference or heard your pastor preach on the topic of sharing the Gospel, you will be familiar with the Great Commission, the command Jesus gave His followers in Mathew 28:18–20 to "go and make disciples of all nations. . . ." Because Jesus said these words, we tend to think of witnessing to all people everywhere as starting in the New Testament. But that is not the case at all—the idea of sharing our faith with "all nations" can be seen throughout the Old Testament. And in many of the psalms we find an impassioned plea for the people of faith to be busy broadcasting the good news of God to people everywhere.

Psalm 150—A Coda of Praise

The Last Song

The book of Psalms is arranged in five books; each book ends with a closing section of praise. In the case of the fifth book, it is not just a verse or two that is used to climax the section in the praise of God but an entire psalm.

Here are the book divisions of the psalms with their respective concluding codas of praise:

- Book 1—Psalms 1–41 (note Psalm 41:13)
- Book 2—Psalms 42–72 (note Psalm 72:18–20)
- Book 3—Psalms 73–89 (note Psalm 89:52)
- Book 4—Psalms 90–106 (note Psalm 106:48)
- Book 5—Psalms 107–150

In book 5, the entire last psalm is the coda of praise; indeed, Psalm 150 is the climax of praise for the entire book of Psalms.

Everything That Has Breath

All the stops are out in Psalm 150. Here is a psalm of joy that reaches to heaven, that includes all of God's people here on earth, and that involves all instruments and voices and even the dance. Without any question, the phrasing of the last verse captures the heart of the psalms and the praise of God: "Let everything that has breath praise the LORD!" (ESV).

In some Bible versions, Psalm 150 begins and ends with the same Hebrew word: *hallelujah*, which is translated "praise the Lord." The word *hallelujah* has penetrated the language wherever the biblical faith has gone. It is one of the words that is known by people all over the world who share an excitement in knowing the God of glory.

This word is made of two elements, the verbal command meaning "praise," plus "Yah" (*jah*), the first part of the divine name Yahweh, a word conventionally rendered as LORD in our English Bibles. The word *hallelujah* means to be excitedly boastful in the Lord. It is certainly a fitting word to conclude our study of some of the psalms of joy: *Hallelujah! Boast joyfully in Yahweh!*

In Summary

What we have chosen to call the psalms of joy are poems of a varied nature from various periods in Israel's experience. They are held together by the emotion of joy, the feeling of happiness in being related to the Lord and in sharing His praise with people.

These are feelings that transcend any Old Testament or New Testament distinction. Believers today join believers of all time in the feeling of joy these psalms present, for this type of joy is known only in the Lord.

Lord, I praise You according to Your excellent greatness! AMEN!

PSALM 63

Because Your lovingkindness is better than life, my lips will praise You.

—Psalm 63:3, NASB1995

I'm independent and, admittedly, stubborn. I'm also a bit of a control freak, so allowing God to lead is difficult for me. Trusting God and releasing worry has been a continual area of growth in my life. That's why this passage from the book of Psalms is so meaningful.

When racing thoughts, worry for my kids, and anxiety over decisions keep me awake at night, I go to the lush meadows in my mind. When health issues threaten my loved ones or me, I imagine drinking from the quiet pools. When I feel overwhelmed by responsibilities, I cling to God's promises, because God knows all my needs— better than I know them. I can trust in God's goodness and mercy.

No matter what I'm facing today, I want to listen to the loving Shepherd, to stop, catch my breath, and let Him send me in the right direction.

—*Missy Tippens*

Notes

Notes

Psalms of Pain

❖————————————❖

*Lord, You are my shield, my glory, and the lifter
of my head.* AMEN.

Feelings

In our last lesson we saw that feelings and emotions are not
only fundamental expressions of our basic humanity, but
they are also central aspects of the book of Psalms. Lesson 2
centered on the psalms of joy. This lesson turns to the darker
moods that are also a part of our humanity.

Even happy people are not always happy; every life is
a mixture of varied feelings and emotions. There are also
moods of pain and anguish. So now we come to what we call
the psalms of pain. This is one of the largest groups of psalms
in the collection. There are more than fifty psalms that fit in
this category. In our lesson now we will focus on Psalm 3.
Then we'll look more briefly at Psalms 4, 5, and 60.

Life Is Tough!

If the psalms of joy are rooted in a radiant sense of the presence of God and His essential goodness, the psalms of pain
are based upon a reality that is also deeply felt: *life is tough!*

Life was tough in biblical days, and it is tough for us today.
One of the splendors of the psalms is the lines of balance

they present in terms of emotional resources. Not all the psalms leave us rejoicing; some provoke our tears. The very fact they might move us to tears, however, is an impetus to work through grief to a sense of relief. When a hurting person discovers that other believers have hurt in similar ways, that person may already be on the way to recovery.

There may be some people who are so isolated in their own little worlds of pleasantries that they can imagine life without struggle. But this is not the case with most of us. It seems to me that most rational people know that life is not easy, that we constantly face pressures and struggles, that outcomes are uncertain, and that, at times, we are very much alone.

The daily routines of life in biblical times must have been quite difficult. Accustomed as we are to all of the technologies, gadgets, and labor-saving devices we take for granted, it is difficult for us to imagine what life might have been like in a small village in Judah in the seventh century BC.

Life in a BC World

Think of it! No cell phones or computers or Internet, no doorstep delivery of packages, supplies, or dinner, no gleaming grocery stores stocked with 100 different kinds of cereal, no over-the-counter cold or pain remedies, no online shopping or streaming TV, no books and magazines, no "smart" microwave ovens or robotic vacuums, and no central heating or A/C.

Houses in Bible times were constructed of stone pillars and mud bricks, with small sleeping quarters above animal stalls. There would have been a smoky fire in the central court for cooking, stone and metal tools for working hides and shaping wood, and looms for making cloth. And beneath the floor were deep cisterns that stored rainwater for family use in the hot, dry summer.

There were no doctors for children's illnesses, no faucets to turn, and no switches to flip. There was scant opportunity for leisure, simply because their work was never done. People then managed flocks rather than worked on computers, and they dealt in trade and barter rather than cash and credit cards. They gathered dung pellets for fuel instead of setting a thermostat for central heating.

War was a constant threat. Not easy-to-put-out-of-mind wars in unseen, distant lands, but brutal person-to-person wars that ravaged their own homes and herds—wars that left many people dead and survivors who might be maimed, raped, impoverished, or enslaved.

We can think about these things, imagine what it was like, and try to put ourselves in their dusty sandals, but not very well. The people of biblical times are remote to us in their manner of life. One thing is for sure, though: even the simplest day was not an easy one for those spiritual ancestors of ours.

Life in Any Day

But it was not these things that provoked the psalms of pain. The relative hardship of living in the ancient world was the norm and the expected. We don't find a psalm of pain that was written because of the drudgery of housework or shepherding!

Doubtless there were significant factors that offset the relative harshness of their daily living. For one thing they had a sense of belonging in place and family that few of us know in today's fast-moving, often-isolated world. They lived close to the land and were sensitive to God, whose benefits may be more readily seen in grassy hillsides than on computer displays.

But always they were people like you and me. Life isn't made up of traffic jams, virtual meetings, or punching the clock any more than their life was merely goat breeding, brick-making, and grain threshing. Life is also the experience of feelings, of emotions. While the trappings of our lives differ from those ancient people, the elemental experiences of human pain and joy are timeless.

Life Closing In

At times their world, like ours, tended to close in all about them. The Hebrew poets use a descriptive term for this pressure in their lives. This is the word *ṣar*.

The word *ṣar* is often translated as "trouble" or "enemy." Its basic meaning is pressure, a closing in, a sense of constraint—no room to breathe. We might associate it today with anxiety or depression. A person experiencing *ṣar* feels alone, alienated, and helpless. The personal hurt seems unbearable, the pressure is unstoppable, and the God who might deliver is unavailable.

The poets who wrote the psalms of pain understood and felt the desperation of the *ṣar* kind of pressure. Their anguish and passion give these psalms their distinctive patterns and moods.

Psalm 3—O Absalom, My Son!

Psalm 3 is an emotional world away from Psalm 33, the poem we studied first in lesson 2. In Psalm 33 there was an air of confidence and a mood of joy that was infectious and compelling. In Psalm 3 we hear another voice; we face another wind. Psalm 3 is a lament, a psalm of pain. We will spend the majority of our lesson in a discussion of this psalm, then briefly survey a few others.

The Superscription

Wherever the psalms have superscriptions—the short, succinct blurb above the psalm text in our Bibles—we will do well to take these notices seriously and use them to inform us in our interpretation. Scholars generally agree that a superscription was not necessarily part of the psalm as it was originally written. More likely, a later editor who collected the psalms for the worship of God in the Temple added the interpretive comments in the superscriptions. (The Dead Sea Scrolls included copies of the psalms dating to the first century that included the superscriptions, so we know that superscriptions dated at least from that time.) The psalms as we have them include the superscriptions. They often form the first verse or two of the poem, and they give us direction in our reading.

The superscription to Psalm 3 puts us squarely in the life of David: "A psalm of David. When he fled from his son Absalom" (NIV). David has been king for some time in Jerusalem. His days of warring with enemy nations are over;

his enemies are either vanquished or vassals, and he is master of an extensive empire.

But David's control over his kingdom in his later years was no stronger than the control he had over his own passions in his younger years. He did not even have complete loyalty in his family.

A Son's Rebellion

One of the saddest stories of the later life of David is the account of the rebellion of his son Absalom. The story is presented with abundant detail in 2 Samuel 13–18. Some of the details are sordid, involving incestuous rape, impassioned fratricide, exile of a son from a father's love, festering rage leading to rebellion of the son against the father, a desperate flight of the king from his throne, the eventual defeat of the son, and the son's rash execution.

All of this is part of the biblical record that, with a few exceptions, describes David as one of the noblest of God's servants. One mark of the excellence of Scripture is the manner in which it never shirks to display the faults of its protagonists, particularly when the record of those faults may be helpful to later readers.

The details of the family history of David are remarkably candid. We have in this story a reminder of the sadness that came into David's life because of the sins against family and honor that broke his career in his affair with Bathsheba and the state murder of Uriah, her husband. We learn that, while God forgave David for his folly, He did not remove from David's life the consequences of his dastardly sin.

Psalm 3 has its setting in the story of David's flight from Jerusalem when Absalom was getting ready to stage a *coup d'état*. The son wanted to make himself king by killing his father (2 Samuel 15:13–16:23). What a desperate situation! The armies of Absalom arrived suddenly; David's flight from Jerusalem was precipitous. Here we have David's cry to God rising from tumultuous sorrow.

So Many!

The first two verses of Psalm 3 focus on the sheer numbers of David's enemies. The word *ṣar*, which we discussed earlier, is found in verse 1 in the phrase "that *trouble* me" (KJV, italics added). Again, the basic idea of this Hebrew word is a constrictive pressure, a loss of breath, a loss of control. Not only does David feel that his enemies are all over him, but he also hears their snarling words mocking his trust in God to deliver him.

Can you imagine such a thing? David's son was his mortal enemy; his son's friends were his foes. In his sense of constriction—in the narrowing of his world—David felt his enemies were innumerable and his own chances for escape from them were nil. This psalm of pain gives much attention to the role of the enemies in the context of David's response to trouble.

A Shield about Me

Only a person of great faith in God could face the pressures David faced in the events surrounding this psalm and then speak as he spoke. The words of verse 3 are unforgettable: "But You, LORD, are a shield around me, my glory, and the One who lifts my head" (NASB).

These words form what we call a confession of trust. They are based on David's prior experience with God and on his knowledge of God through the Torah, the written Word of God.

There are times when life seems hopeless, and there seems to be no escape from the distress and pressures that press in on us. It is then we have the opportunity to display resilient faith in God, who never leaves us but is always near.

In his words of trust in this verse, David draws upon the military imagery of his day. With no weapon and with enemies all about him, he seized on the idea that he may still live, that there is still hope. He pictures God as a great shield—invisible but impenetrable.

Alone and despondent, David now realizes he is safe. And because God has spared him, he is now also able to raise his head again. Along the way, he has been reminded that his true sense of significance, his genuine glory, is not in himself, but in his relationship to God. So he affirms that the Lord has heard his prayer, that his words have rushed headlong into heaven, and that God is listening (verse 4).

To Sleep, Perchance to Dream

When a person is really upset or despondent, it is sometimes impossible to sleep. Lying in bed, unable to sleep despite great fatigue, is a misery many people face from time to time. Apparently, David had been unable to sleep, and the reason may well have been his anxiety over the rebellion of his son and his own need to escape from Jerusalem. But when he acknowledged the protection of the Lord and that He had heard his prayer, David was able to lie down and sleep (verse 5). And the reason David was able to sleep, even in the midst of great adversity, is that he had rediscovered the protective presence of God. He had been given room to breathe again.

Arise, O Lord

Now in verses 6–8, David is prepared to trust in the Lord to restore his own fortunes as well as to destroy the enemies who have harassed him. And so David is able to sleep. Then in the morning he awakens and senses the protective presence of the Lord. It is almost as though he says, "Bring on my enemies! I am not afraid of them anymore." The reference to fearlessness in the presence of "ten thousands" (verse 6) stands in direct contrast to his timidity at the beginning of the psalm, when he was overcome by the sheer numbers of his enemies (verses 1–2). Even though the circumstances haven't changed yet, David is confident they will. The transformation is complete.

Strike My Enemies

And in renewed faith, David turns to God and asks Him to destroy his enemies. In a vivid word picture, the second half of verse 7 asks God to "strike all my enemies on the jaw; break the teeth of the wicked" (NIV).

Here is another example that illustrates the difficulty of translating the Hebrew verbs in the psalms. With all that we've learned in recent years, we are far better able to translate the time factors than were the translators who worked on the King James Version more than 400 years ago. While the King James translated the verbs here in past tense, as already having done or completed ("Thou has smitten"; "Thou hast broken"), most recent versions translate them as imperatives (which Merriam-Webster defines as words "expressive of . . . entreaty"), carrying out the idea of the beginning of verse 7: "Arise, LORD! Deliver me, my God!" (NIV).

In the Chops!

The call for blows against the cheek and the teeth in verse 7 has its basis in animal imagery. The strong jaws and sharp teeth of a fearsome beast like a lion are symbols of its power. When David asks God to strike his enemies in the mouth, he is asking for an end to their destructive force. It is as though he is saying, "Hit them in the chops; defang them!"

These harsh words introduce to us the concept of the imprecation, or cursing one's enemies, in the psalms. It is likely most of us are uncomfortable with this kind of strong language. One reason for this might be that we have been led to believe, or intuitively suspect, that the Bible will always speak of sweetness and light, not of nastiness and darkness. Further, we have ringing in our ears the words of Jesus to forgive our enemies and even to turn the other cheek.

Why These Curses?

Frequently, people find it difficult to reconcile the beautifully descriptive words of Psalm 23:1, "the Lord is my shepherd," with such harsh words as "strike all my enemies on the jaw; break the teeth of the wicked" (verse 7, NIV). This is a puzzling anomaly that we cannot avoid confronting because it shows up again and again in the psalms.

Old Testament Curses?

The distinctions of the loving and vindictive passages in the psalms are not to be viewed simply on a moral level or as spiritual insight. For instance, it isn't that a psalm like Psalm 23 breathes the spirit of the New Testament and Psalm 3 reflects the spirit of the Old Testament. It is certainly not that God in the Old Testament was less kind than Jesus in the New. To think that way would be to have a deficient view of God and of His Word, as well as a prejudgment of proper behavior that brings the text under the judgment of the reader, rather than the reader under the judgment of the text.

Three Ideas in the Cursings

There are several factors that are involved in explaining the concept of the imprecations found in the psalms. Basically, there are three ideas that work together in the cursings:

- The Psalmists' identification with God
- The ongoing continuity of the covenant
- A pattern for future fulfillment

  Here is a brief survey of these ideas.

An Attack on God

First, these imprecations are not just the personal pique or outrage of the Psalmist. Neither are they petty attempts at getting even, an extension of what might be called "playground behavior." The Psalmists, particularly David, have so identified themselves with the Lord and with His work that an attack on Him is really an attack on the person of God. We remember that David is the regent of the Lord over Israel.

Now, it should be obvious that for any of us today to take this kind of extreme position would be dangerous. But in his time David was justified in thinking as he did. The people who drove him out of Jerusalem, his capital city, were not just rejecting him as their king; they were actually attacking God through David. And they deserved punishment for their sin. Since David was the Lord's anointed, to attack him was to attack his God.

God's Covenant with Abraham

A second factor in our understanding of these imprecations in the psalms is rooted in the basic covenant that the Lord made with Abraham (then Abram) in Genesis 12:1–3. Included among the several provisions of that covenant were these words: "I will bless those who bless you, and whoever curses you I will curse" (NIV).

When David asks God to bring divine wrath on his enemies, he is invoking the privilege of covenant; he is saying, "Your will be done." When enemies of Israel rose up against them, the covenant promise was that these enemies would come under the judgment of God.

A Portent of the Future

A third aspect to the pronouncement of the curse of God on the enemies of David is prophetic in nature. As little as we like the idea of wrath and judgment in the psalms, a greater wrath and judgment than we can imagine awaits evil people who reject God. It is easy to forget that there is a New Testament–based Christian, biblical basis for a final judgment, found in 2 Timothy 4:1: "the Lord Jesus Christ . . . shall judge the quick [the living] and the dead at his appearing and his kingdom" (KJV).

Old and New?

This simply means that we cannot really contrast the "lower, Old Testament" view of God's wrath with the "higher, New Testament" picture of a gentle Jesus—and remain genuinely biblical. The gentle Jesus, meek and mild, that so many people picture is a product of their own imagining; He is not the Jesus of Scripture, or at least not the whole of the Jesus of Scripture. For He who cradled children lovingly in His arms (Mark 10:16) is also the one who promises ultimate judgment to those who reject Him (Matthew 24–25).

The Apostle Paul put his finger on the New Testament understanding of "the wrath of God" when he wrote, "For the wrath of God is revealed from heaven *against all ungodliness and unrighteousness of men, who by their unrighteousness suppress the truth*" (Romans 1:18, ESV; italics added). Here we see that God's "wrath" is directed toward those who finally reject Him. Paul's point is that God's wrath doesn't mean that He is angry at us. Rather, Paul is saying that the wrath of God is, in a sense, our self-inflicted pain, the result of our willful sin.

At the same time, we have assurance of the eternal truth that God has no desire to be wrathful or to exact punishment. A late New Testament writer illuminates this truth when he says, "The Lord is not slow in keeping his promise, as some understand slowness. Instead he is *patient with you, not wanting anyone to perish*, but everyone to come to repentance" (2 Peter 3:9, NIV; italics added).

In the psalms, though, the relevance of final judgment to the cursings is one of ultimate fulfillment. The cursings that David directed toward his enemies were not always fulfilled. Sometimes they were the expression of his own desire, but we may suspect that only occasionally did his words result in the destruction of his enemies. But there is an overarching theme to biblical cursings: one day, all wicked people will be judged by a righteous God. As we have seen, the Bible presents life and death issues as they are, not as we might like them to be.

What about Us?

This raises a question. If we accept the idea that it may have been all right for David to pronounce curses against his enemies, does that leave the door open for us to follow his example?

The immediate answer is no. Here are some reasons:

- It may be that an attack on us is prompted by an attack on God, but that is far less likely than in David's case, for he filled a unique role as God's regent. Usually an attack on us is prompted by simpler reasons.

- The covenant aspects are also problematic. We usually understand the covenant protection to relate to Hebrew and Jewish people. Such being the case it is difficult to extend these covenant provisions to Christian believers in the same way.

- There is a distinction between believing in the reality of the future judgment and actually praying for that judgment to come.

Jesus told His followers, "Love your enemies, bless them that curse you, do good to them that hate you, and pray for them which despitefully use you, and persecute you" (Matthew 5:44, KJV).

Mercy, Not Judgment

This simply means that as Christian believers, we are not to pray for God's judgment to strike those who oppose us. There are just too many uncertainties, too many risks to pray that way. We most certainly can pray that our enemies will change (perhaps this is what Jesus meant when He said to pray for our enemies), that their intended evil will not succeed, and that they will receive the Lord and be saved.

And with that, we must leave final judgment to the Lord. We will do well to heed the word of the Old Testament Hebrew writer: "Vengeance is Mine" (Deuteronomy 32:35, NASB). It was this that the Apostle Paul picked up on when he wrote, "Never take your own revenge, beloved, but leave room for the wrath of God, for it is written: 'VENGEANCE IS MINE, I WILL REPAY,' says the Lord" (Romans 12:19, NASB). And this same theme is echoed by one of the psalms writers: "O LORD, God of vengeance, O God of vengeance, shine forth!" (Psalm 94:1, ESV).

Summary

This rather lengthy digression in which we've taken a closer look at the cursings of enemies in the Old Testament was necessary to gain a biblical balance to the issue. The idea of calling down judgment on enemies is not an isolated phenomenon in Scripture. Rather, it is a part of a larger whole that includes the majesty and holiness of God, the actions of

God in behalf of His covenant community, and the purpose of God in final judgment.

The Structure of the Psalms of Pain (Lament)

The structure of the psalms of pain is somewhat complex, usually containing the following elements:

- An opening cry ("O my God!")
- The lament of pain (using three pronouns)

    I am hurting.

    You do not care.

    They are winning.

- A confession of trust
- The petition (using three verbs)

    Hear me!

    Save me!

    Punish them!

- A vow of praise

    Let's explain these elements briefly.

O My God!

The opening cry is a call for help that is based on a prior relationship with the Lord. That is, this is not just the glib exclamation we hear people uttering out of shock or in a time of trouble; it is the deliberate use of the words, "O my God."

I, You, They

The lament is the cry of distress, where the Psalmist states in somewhat startling language the extent of his trouble. This is experiential language, sometimes exaggerated for effect, but always expressing the deep feelings of the Psalmist. It has three parts, each using a pronoun:

- "I am hurting!" Here the writer may express in some detail the nature of his pain. The source of his pain could be illness, emotional distress, a physical attack in times of war, or countless other sources. The general nature of the setting in many of the psalms of pain allows us to fill in our own particulars.
- "You don't care!" The most outrageous aspect of these psalms, perhaps even more troubling than the calls for the cursing of one's enemies, is the charge against God that He is uninterested in the pain of the Psalmist. Again, this is the language of experience. This is what the Psalmist feels, what he thinks is happening. It is a marvel of the poetry of the Bible that such genuine feelings, even when they present challenges to God, would be included.
- "They are winning!" By these words, the Psalmist describes the ascendancy of his enemies, a factor that makes his own hopeless condition bleaker. Again, the enemies may or may not be specified.

These three pronouns are not always present in the psalm, nor are they necessarily balanced in emphasis. For example, in Psalm 3 there is a focus on "they" and a minimizing of the other two elements. But it is not unusual in the psalms of pain for all three pronouns of the lament to be prominent.

But in You I Trust
If the psalm ended in the words of lament, it would be a dia-tribe or a maudlin exercise—a giving up to depression and a

turning away from the Lord. In the psalms of pain there will always be a confession of trust that will balance the expression of lament or pain. In this interplay there is an accurate reflection of our feelings in times of trouble and of our deep beliefs and convictions. There is a war within; our experience at the moment is in conflict with our faith and conviction.

Hear! Save! Punish!

The confession of trust then leads to the petition—the requests that are made of God in the context of great pain. Often the petition has three prominent verbs—the Psalmist asks God to *hear* his prayer, to *save* him from his distress, and to *punish* his enemies.

As we look at this outline, we will discover that there are some natural linkages between the lament and the petition. These may be related in this manner:

Lament	*Petition*
I am hurting.	Save me!
You don't care.	Hear me!
They are winning.	Punish them!

As the verbs "hear" and "save" relate to the troubles of the Psalmist, so the verb "punish" relates to the troublers themselves. There is a satisfying sense of closure in these psalms as we see the potential for a movement toward the end of a problem.

I Will Pay My Vow

There may at times be certain additional elements in these psalms of pain. Sometimes there are some reasons given for the Lord to listen to the prayer of the tormented writer.

We will see one example of this when we study Psalm 6. But the psalms will regularly conclude on the note of praise. If the Psalmist has not yet been delivered from the distress he describes at the beginning, he will conclude his psalm with a promise to the Lord that when he is delivered from his trouble, he will go to the center of worship and tell everyone what God did to save him. He will make his public proclamation of the praise of God.

Sometimes we will find a report of deliverance somewhere in the psalm. In those cases, the Psalmist will record his words of praise at the end of the psalm. In either instance, the psalms of pain end as psalms of joy. Lament always turns to praise in the Hebrew psalms.

With this explanation in mind, let's take a look at a few more of the psalms of pain.

Psalm 4—To Lie Down in Peace

A Follow-up—in Confidence

Psalm 4 has several similarities to Psalm 3, leading some interpreters to believe that both of them may have been inspired by the same experience in David's life. However, this psalm of pain has a great deal more confidence in it than we found in Psalm 3. Perhaps this psalm is a follow-up to David's prayer in Psalm 3 while he was still under assault from his son Absalom.

In this brief poem, there is the introductory cry for help in verse 1, followed immediately by words of confession and petition. There is barely any note of lament at all.

A Confession of Trust

Verse 3 is a powerful statement of confident trust in the Lord. The Psalmist is addressing his enemies in this verse, and if this poem is linked to Psalm 3, then these are words of a father to a rebellious son and to those who are allied with him. "But know that the LORD has set apart the godly person for Himself; the LORD hears when I call to Him" (NASB).

Here David is reflecting on his special call and anointing as the regent of the Lord, the true king of Israel. He is making it clear that anyone who attacks him should know what they are up against, for God Himself has set him aside in a special place of significance and leadership. It is not a small thing to attack one who has been anointed by the Lord.

When we read these words, we find encouragement for our own pilgrimage of faith. This verse doesn't just relate to someone in ancient Israel. Rather, these words apply to all true believers at any time. As Christians we receive special care and protection from God. This doesn't mean that we will not experience hard times and suffering, but it does mean that we have positive assurance that God hears us when we call out to Him.

An Appeal of Mercy

Perhaps the most remarkable thing about Psalm 4 is the attitude David now expresses toward his enemies. As we contrast the spirit expressed in this psalm with that of Psalm 3, we catch a glimpse of the marvelous balance of attitudes. Whereas in Psalm 3 God was asked to strike out at the writer's enemies, this psalm makes an appeal to evil men to turn away from their sin and place their trust in God.

Verse 2 is a direct challenge to sinful and pagan people to abandon their wicked ways, to turn away from their worship of false gods and worship the one true God. Verse 3, as we've already noted, is an affirmation of the care and protection that God's people can enjoy.

Verses 4 and 5 offer a direct appeal to sinful and rebellious people to give up their evil ways: "Tremble [with anger or fear], and do not sin" (4:4, AMP). They are urged to spend time alone in the privacy of their rooms and take an honest look at the evil and sin in their lives: "Meditate in your heart upon your bed and be still [reflect on your sin and repent of your rebellion]" (4:4, AMP). And once they acknowledge their sin, they can put their faith in the Lord and join other true believers in worshipping Him.

We have in this psalm a genuine expression of mercy—a true statement of the gospel that calls for an inner change, for trust in the Lord. It is then and only then people can experience peace with God. The Psalmist, who already enjoys that peace, then concludes the psalm with his personal affirmation: "In peace I will both lie down and sleep; for you alone, O LORD, make me dwell in safety" (4:8, ESV).

Psalm 5—Evil Words from Evil Men

Another innovation in the psalms of pain comes in Psalm 5. The distinctives of this particular poem show that the pattern we have discussed so far is not cast into a fixed mold.

This is a psalm of lament that speaks of a most distressing period in the Psalmist's life, a time when he was besieged by enemies that were pitted against him. But in this instance his enemies were attacking with the weapons of speech. They resorted to lies, deceit, and flattery. In colorful language, the Psalmist described them this way: "For there is nothing trustworthy in their mouth; their inward part is destruction itself. Their throat is an open grave; they flatter with their tongue" (5:9, NASB).

Sticks and Stones . . . and Words

The old bromide about sticks and stones not really hurting is nonsense, as everyone who has felt the sharp barb of spiteful words readily knows. From the young child who endures playground teasing, to the teenager who is the butt of incessant taunting on social media, to the adult who is under debilitating duress because of the cutting words of another person—evil words do hurt. Sometimes these negative words hurt more intensely and for a much longer time than a physical blow.

In the culture of the Old Testament, however, more is involved than just the use of bad and cutting words. In the world of the psalms, words were believed to "speak"; that is, the use of language for blessing or for cursing was more than just something pleasant or unpleasant. It was an invocation of the gods (or of God) to actually do what the words called for. It was believed that curses hurled in invective had some kind of divine power that would make happen what was called for.

In Psalm 5 the Psalmist is in distress because of the lying, boastful lips of his adversaries (see especially verses 4–6, 9–10). The words of cursing bring out sharply the principal issue: it is not just that an attack has been made on David, but that the people who are his foes have rebelled against the Lord (verse 10).

The Righteous One

In this psalm, the personality of the Psalmist is clearly seen. But there is still something that is distinctive to the psalm, for the person of the Psalmist is so closely linked to the person of God that the Psalmist seems to move back and forth from one to the other with relative ease. Ultimately, the psalm points to the person of Jesus Christ. It is He whom the Psalmist ultimately describes as the Righteous in verse 12: "Surely, Lord, you bless the righteous; you surround them with your favor as with a shield" (NIV). And God's people in all time share in that blessing. It is this expectation that helps us to live in troubled times with a proper perspective.

Psalm 60—A Psalm of Military Disaster

The superscription to Psalm 60 relates it to certain campaigns of David's in Edom, Moab, and Philistia (2 Samuel 8 and 1 Chronicles 18). While the psalm itself does not identify specific times or occasions, it is clear from this psalm of pain that Israel had suffered a devastating military defeat. As a result of this humiliating disaster, the Psalmist describes the ravaged landscape as being comparable to the aftereffects of a great earthquake.

As the Psalmist works his way through the poem, we see him in verses 6–8 seeming to remind God that He had promised better things for His people. The tragedy of the moment didn't seem to square with their view and hope for the future. But then, as the Psalmist moved toward the close of his poem, we hear him pray, "Give us aid against the enemy, for human help is worthless" (60:11, NIV). And with that prayer came a special insight, for with a fresh breath of hope, the writer then says, "With God we shall do valiantly; it is he who will tread down our foes" (60:12, ESV).

From hopelessness to hope. This is our heritage in Jesus Christ. There is no trouble so great or devastation so complete that God can't provide a way through. Pay special attention to this truth: the Christian has no promise of being free from the pain that is a part of this life. We will have our struggles and our hard times. There will be those moments when we feel as if all is lost. Yet we can share with confidence the faith of the three young men in Babylon who refused to be overwhelmed by the fiery furnace and said boldly, "Our God whom we serve is able to deliver us" (Daniel 3:17, KJV).

In Summary

There is a pattern used in the psalms of pain that is somewhat elaborate and flexible. When we understand the basic idea of the pattern, some of the unusual features of these varied psalms will make more sense to us. We will know what to expect, and we will also be prepared for the variations that the individual poem presents for effect.

The most significant thing to remember in these psalms is that they do not wallow in sorrow or linger long in the mood of pain in which they begin. In most instances the Psalmist moves from agonizing expressions of pain to exuberant praise of God. All of the psalms are to be read and used for worship and praise—even the psalms of pain.

Lord, help me always trust in You as the Psalmist
trusted in You; even in the most difficult times,
I know You are always with me. AMEN.

PSALM 5

But as for me, I will enter Your house through the abundance of Your steadfast love and tender mercy; at Your holy temple I will bow [obediently] in reverence for You.

—Psalm 5:7, AMP

I love this verse. And I think the reason I love it so much is that I often come to the Lord empty. Empty-handed, with nothing to bring Him, and also empty down in my soul, with a painful longing to be satisfied, and yet the knowledge that I have absolutely nothing to offer in the exchange. There's not a single, solitary reason He would want to let me enter His house. And yet. The Bible says I can enter through the abundance of His steadfast love and mercy.

I picture myself, this grubby pauper lifting a stained hand to knock on the door. But even before I can knock, the door is thrown open wide and my Father steps forward to greet me.

This relationship is a great mystery: how we can be loved with the familiarity of a family, totally secure knowing He is always with us and yet loved by a holy being who's so very different from us. His ways are past finding out. He is high and lifted up. He is totally different— beyond our comprehension.

When I come to the Lord, one thing He gives me in exchange for my emptiness is awe. An awe that someone like Him would come to earth to save someone like me. What a mystery. What a Savior!

—*Gwen Ford Faulkenberry*

Notes

Notes

Psalms of the Wise

*Lord, help me to walk not in the counsel of the
ungodly, or stand with sinners, or sit with the scornful.
Let me delight in Your Word.* AMEN.

Prophets, Priests, and Kings

Generally, when we think of the varied positions of important people in the Bible, three basic categories come to mind:
prophet, priest, and king. Not all the prominent people
in the biblical story were members of these groups, but
certainly many can be found in one of these three positions.
So we will begin this part of our study by reflecting on these
three groups.

The prophet was the spokesperson for God to the people.
Some of the prophets were women; most were men. They
were called by God to announce His message to the people.
Often this was a message of judgment because of their revolt
against His covenant by worshipping pagan gods. At times,
the prophets also spoke words of blessing and promise. Some
of the most magnificent of these promise oracles center on
the coming of the One we speak of today as the Messiah, the
Lord Jesus Christ. The prophets were both forthtellers and
foretellers. That is, they spoke to the people and their settings

first, and they also looked into the future in specific, predictive ways.

The priest, who in Israel could only be a man, was a mediator between God and the people in their religious practices. The priest was regarded as being outside of secular, lay society. He was a man under orders. The priest was holy—that is, distinct, other, set apart. Only the priest could serve within the sacred areas of the Tabernacle or Temple.

There were gradations of responsibility and rank among the priests. The highest in rank was the high priest. Only he could enter the Holiest Place within the Tabernacle or Temple, and even then on just one occasion each year—the Day of Atonement, or Yom Kippur. On that auspicious day, the high priest would enter what was regarded as the earthly dwelling of God and make atonement for the people.

In biblical times, a lay person usually needed to go through a priest to have access to God. In addition to supervising the sacrifices in the Temple, priests were also men of learning. Priests were scholars of the Law of God and the teachers of its meaning to the people.

The king was the civil leader of Israel, but he also served a religious role. He was to represent God to the people, to guide them in righteousness, to give aid to the helpless, and to protect the weak. This ideal was rarely realized fully in life, but the ideal was always maintained in principle. The king was to be an agent for good for the people, not a means of their hurt or his own gain. He was to be a father to his people, a hero in war, an adjudicator in disputes, and an instrument for peace.

The Offices and the Messiah

These three positions or institutions—prophet, priest, and king—were most significant in ancient Israel. Each of them also served as a portrait of what the coming Messiah would be like. For the coming One was to be a Prophet who was superior to Moses, a Priest who was superior to Aaron, and a King who was superior to David. For this reason, we may describe the Lord Jesus as Prophet, Priest, and King.

The Sage

But there is another category of persons that is not often mentioned—the sage or the wise person. The model for the sage in ancient Israel is Solomon in the early days of his reign as king. You remember that Solomon succeeded his father, David, as king and is closely associated with the wisdom books of the Bible, such as Proverbs and Ecclesiastes.

The sage was not anointed as was a prophet, priest, or king, but the role of the sage was common in Israel as well as in other countries of the ancient Near East. The sage or wise person was a man or a woman who devoted his or her life to observation, reflection, thought, and teaching. When a sage was godly, his or her wisdom was thoroughly integrated with the knowledge and fear of the Lord.

Now, just as there were godly priests, prophets, and kings, so, too, were there ungodly ones who perverted their offices. At one point in his preaching the prophet Jeremiah indicated that his enemies included the priests, the wise persons, and the prophets (Jeremiah 18:18). This verse is significant in the way it includes the wise along with priests and prophets.

Tabletalk Magazine
Ligonier Ministries
421 Ligonier Ct.
Sanford, FL 32771

Periodicals

Significant portions of the Bible come from the wise. The principal wisdom books are Proverbs, Job, Ecclesiastes, and several psalms, particularly the ones we consider in this lesson: 1, 8, 14, 78, 119, and 139.

Psalm 1

The Beginning of the Psalms

We have delayed looking at Psalm 1 until this lesson so that we could group it with other psalms of its category. Yet it is fitting for the book of Psalms to begin with this poem. We don't know who wrote it or when it was composed, but that doesn't matter.

Psalm 1 is not the call to praise God that we might expect at the beginning of the book of Praises (the meaning of the Hebrew title for the psalms). Rather, Psalm 1 is a call to contemplate the Word of God. It is as though the organizers of the book of Psalms felt that before we really are able to praise the Lord rightly, we need to know who He is and what He does. And the place to learn that is first in His Word and then in His works. The wisdom writers direct us to both.

The Style of the Wise

Psalm 1 is distinct from those we have studied up to this point. It has a different mood than either a psalm of joy or a psalm of pain. It has style, polished rhetoric, and panache. It is also filled with contrasts of good and evil and with a special interest in the Torah, the Word of God. We might better expect to locate Psalm 1 in the book of Proverbs. It is not so much a song as a poetic essay or editorial. It is, in a

way, a doorway to the music of the Bible, but that doorway is
marked by certain warnings and significant blessings.

A Blessing on the Righteous

Psalm 1 has two parts. Verses 1–3 focus on God's blessing
on the righteous; verses 4–6 speak of His judgment of the
wicked. It is the pattern for the wise in Israel to make blanket
contrasts—there is no middle ground in these categories. The
righteous are made up of those who believe in the Lord and
who center their lives upon Him and His Word. The wicked
are those who have rejected the Lord, who barely give Him a
thought, and whose lives may mirror their godlessness.

Blessed

Psalm 1 begins with the word "blessed." This word reminds
us of the words of Jesus in the opening of the Sermon on the
Mount (Matthew 5:3–11), the Beatitudes. There He pro-
nounces His blessing on people, some of whom have suffered
greatly for their defense of God's truth in a wicked world. In
fact, the Beatitudes of Jesus in the Sermon on the Mount are
based on and are a development of the beatitudes we find in
the wisdom books of the Old Testament. Jesus is the Wise as
well as Prophet, Priest, and King.

The Hebrew word translated "blessed" in Psalm 1:1 is a
word of significant power. It may be translated, "How very
happy!" In this we have a reminder of the psalms of joy in
lesson 2. It is interesting to be reminded that the Bible has
a great deal to say about authentic happiness. Happiness—
joy—is our birthright as Christians. Contrary to the dour and

pained attitude that has become stereotypical of Christian society, Jesus reflected joy and happiness.

Progressive Participation

The words of the psalms work together in the poetic patterns we term "parallelism." This was touched on in "An Overview of Psalms." Psalm 1 is an excellent example of how this works. There are three elements in the first verse, each with the understood preface, "Blessed is the one who does not . . ." These speak of progressive involvement in wickedness. First, "Blessed is the one who does not walk in step with the wicked." This person will not be associated with sin and wickedness. Second, "Blessed is the one who does not . . . stand in the way that sinners take." This person is not comfortable standing, or sitting, with sinful people and refuses to participate in their activities. Third, "Blessed is the one who does not . . . sit in the company of mockers" (NIV). This is the person who is not only involved with evil and sinful people but mocks scornfully the ways of God and the people of God.

In the synthetic or progressive parallelism of the first verse of this psalm, the writer warns the believer to stay clear of the slippery slope that leads to spiritual disaster. Consequently, the words in this verse contain a benediction—a blessing—on the person who does not walk with, stand or sit with, or join in the contemptuous attitudes of wicked and sinful people.

In His Law

Now, the negative mood of verse 1 is a foil for the positive words the Psalmist expresses in verse 2, "but his delight is in the law of the LORD, and on his law he meditates day and night" (ESV).

First, it is helpful to understand that the term "law" in this verse is not restricted to some arcane obligations or restrictions from the ancient, or modern, world. The meaning is much broader than that, as a rule, when used in the Bible.

The Hebrew *torah* is one of the principal words to describe the Bible as God's revelation. The word *Torah* is used first for the Pentateuch—Genesis, Exodus, Leviticus, Numbers, and Deuteronomy—as the basic texts for God's message to His people. But then the word takes on a more general sense that includes the whole Bible. It is all Torah, for it is all revelation from God.

Basically, the Hebrew word *torah* means "direction" or "instruction." The word is like a pictorial display of the intentions God has for His people. It may be compared to a pointed index finger marking out the way. It is God showing His people how to live in relationship to Him. The word *law* in English does not convey all of these ideas. This is the reason many Jewish scholars suggest not translating this word, but transliterating it into English and then explaining its meaning, much as we have done here.

Verse 2 is the heart of the psalm. A truly godly person finds his or her deepest enjoyment in the study of and meditation on the Word of God. This is not because we worship a book. It is not because we have some unnatural preoccupation with words. And it is certainly not because we believe that by long study we may earn favor with God.

Rather, the coming in joy to the Word of God is prompted because of what we learn there about Him. Pure and simple, this is it: in the study of His Word, we are drawn more closely to God.

Now, the Word of God is not the only means of being drawn closer to Him. We can also be drawn closer to God through an appreciation of and experience in the world that He has created. Then, too, we can grow nearer to Him by means of regular prayer and communion and in the participation of community worship. The psalms deal with all of these. In lesson 6 we will explore the psalms of nature, for example, and we have already looked closely at the psalms of joy and the psalms of pain, which speak of the individual and collective experiences we have in our pilgrimage of faith.

But it is the Word of God that is primary. The reason is simple: only by means of the Word of God can we evaluate properly the other experiences we may have. We may look at a great sequoia tree, for example, in the forests of Northern California and be drawn in our thoughts to the Creator. But another person may look at that same tree and have no thought of God whatsoever. What makes the difference? The answer is in the lenses through which we look—the Word of God.

Similarly, we may be involved in a wonderfully emotional experience in singing words of praise to God among a community of worshippers. But another person in the same room might be singing the same words of a praise song but be thinking on a wavelength a world away from biblical faith. Then, too, to some people words like love and peace and joy might speak to a brand of religious thought that has nothing directly to do with the truth of God as revealed in Jesus Christ. What makes the difference? The answer again is in the discriminating understanding we gain in the study of the Word of God.

Like a Tree

It is to be expected that poetry of all languages will make abundant use of figures of speech. Certainly the poetry of the Bible uses words in creative, pictorial ways. A superb example of this is seen in the image of the tree in verse 3. Persons who have centered their lives in God and who have avoided being associated with sinful actions and people are "like a tree."

It is helpful to understand that the tree the Psalmist has in mind is not an evergreen or deciduous tree like those that populate most of North America. The tree referred to here is a date-producing variety of the desert palm. The poet, whose name isn't known, gives us a vivid description of the tree and its setting. And as he paints word pictures of this tree, he makes colorful comparisons with the blessings of righteous people who are faithful to God:

- ". . . a tree planted by streams of water" (NASB). It has an abundance of water, and this reminds us of nourishment. The Psalmist has already said that the proper nourishment for the soul of a righteous person is found in the Word of God.
- ". . . which yields its fruit in its season." The picture here is of a fruit-bearing date palm. This speaks of productivity— fruitfulness—in the life of the believer. Christians whose lives are centered in the Word of God are productive like

a fruit-bearing palm. As Christians, by words and actions, we are to witness to our faith by feeding the hungry, giving water to the thirsty, being friendly to strangers, providing clothing to those in need, visiting the sick and those in prison, and telling people everywhere the good news of the Gospel (Matthew 25:35–36; 28:19–20).

- "... its leaf does not wither." This is a tree that never drops its fronds or leaves. There are signs of life year-round. Unlike deciduous trees that appear lifeless during the winter season, this tree always looks alive. We never mistake a dead palm tree for a live one. The comparison here is obvious—the believer always reflects the alive Spirit of the living God.

- The tree is valuable. The phrase "... and in whatever he does, he prospers" has been interpreted by some to be a blanket guarantee of business and financial success in life. But God doesn't make such guarantees. Instead, the idea expressed here is a life of usefulness and purpose. Even as there are many different uses for the desert palm, so the follower of God is to be a person who is useful in the work of the Lord.

Like Chaff

"Not so the wicked! They are like chaff that the wind blows away" (verse 4, NIV). Not only does this verse begin the second division of the psalm, but it also gives a dramatic contrast to the tree image. Unlike righteous and obedient people, those who refuse to follow the Lord are like chaff, a messy and useless by-product of the useful and nourishing grain. In ancient times in threshing season a winnowing tool would be used to toss the grain in the air so the breeze or wind would blow the light and useless chaff away, separating it from the grain.

Then in verse 5 the analogy is carried to its logical conclusion. The ungodly, the chaff, do not endure the judgment of God. And verse 6 continues the theme with a complex antithetical parallelism, "For the LORD watches over the way of the righteous, but the way of the wicked leads to destruction" (NIV). Here we have the affirmation of the righteous and the rejection of the ungodly.

Because the way of the ungodly perishes, the way of the righteous endures; because the Lord knows the way of the righteous, He does not know (in the sense of being related to) the way of the wicked. This verse shows the added dimensions to meaning that an understanding of parallelism brings to our reading of the psalms.

Psalm 1 and Jesus

The focus of Psalm 1 is primarily on a righteous person whose life is in full conformity to the Word of God. When we reflect on that, we realize that even the best Christians only approximate the ideals of the wisdom writer of this psalm. A righteous person might come nearer the ideal pictured here, but no one can measure up to the ideals expressed in this psalm.

Except One. When we think of the righteous person in the wisdom writings of the psalms, we are inevitably led to think of the Lord Jesus Christ. This is not to say that this is necessarily a psalm that looks ahead to the coming of Jesus as some of them seem to. But there is a flow of biblical thought, a direction of biblical history, that leads us inexorably from the righteous person of Psalm 1 to the Righteous One, the Lord Jesus Christ. We may expect to find this same flow of thought in other psalms of the wise. In many and varied ways, the psalms lead us to the Savior.

Psalm 8—The Majesty of Humankind

God's Majestic Name

Psalm 8 is another wisdom psalm, and it is laced with dramatic theology. As you will note, the psalm begins and ends with the same wording, an exultation of the majesty of God and the excellence of His name in all creation. Verses 1 and 9 read, "LORD, our LORD, how majestic is Your name in all the earth, You who have displayed Your splendor above the heavens!" (NASB). These majestic words provide a frame for the Psalmist's central message, and they are words that might well frame our days. One wonders if we repeated them first thing in the morning and last thing at night, whether the hours in between would take on a whole new flavor.

The body of the psalm has the following simple structure:

- An affirmation of praise to God who is the Creator of all things and whose rule is not affected by opposition in any form (verses 1–2)
- A discovery of the significance of man, who, as male and female, has the highest place in God's creation (verses 3–8)

God's Highest Praise

The first section of the psalm is reminiscent of the psalms of joy. The focus is on the praise of God, whose glory is above the heavens and who receives praises even from toddlers as He scoffs at anyone who might represent himself as His foe.

The wording of verses 1 and 2 is quite difficult in the original Hebrew and has commanded a great deal of attention by scholars. In plain and simple language free of trappings, these verses read something like this: "God is to be praised as the Creator of the universe. He will be praised—if only by children. (In fact, Jesus suggested one day that if people will not give God the praise He insists upon, He will accept it from stones!) Enemies mean nothing in the presence of God, and a foe of God is a joke but the humor is grisly."

God's Finest Work

The surprise in this psalm comes in verses 3–8. This section is shaped in the form of a dramatic soliloquy, a discussion within, a meditation on the nature of reality.

The Psalmist presents himself as looking into the night sky and finding himself quite overcome by the stars (verse 3). Often in our city air, the night sky is compromised not only by haze but also by a million points of little lights. But every once in a while, away from the glare of city lights, we are able to rediscover the heavens.

A trip to one of America's incredible national parks, with their wide-open vistas and lack of manmade lights, will show us a sky alive with myriad stars that are invisible in our normal circumstances. And like the Psalmist, in a setting like that we can't help being overwhelmed by our smallness in the big picture of God's creation and, in turn, by how trivial our planet earth is in the vastness of the universe. What could we possibly mean to a God who has made all this? The writer wondered why too: "What is mankind that you are mindful of them, human beings that you care for them?" (verse 4, NIV).

God and Angels

The Psalmist's response to those questions staggers the imagination. You are probably familiar with the King James Version's wording of the first part of verse 5 that says that God has made man "a little lower than the angels." If this were the correct translation of this verse, it would be significant, wouldn't it? We think of angels as spirit beings who are in close proximity to God, serving as His messengers and ministers in heaven.

But that translation falls short. The Hebrew word in verse 5 is not "angels" but "God." The Hebrew word for angels looks nothing like the word that is used here. Many modern translations use "God" in place of "the angels." When we read it that way, it can be quite startling! "You have made him a little lower than God, and You crown him with glory and majesty!" (NASB).

In God's Image

As we read the rest of the verses of the psalm, we find language that takes us back to the story of Creation in the book of Genesis. Here we have affirmed again in verses 6–8 that we are in charge of God's creation. It was this mandate that was given to humankind by God in Genesis 1:26–28.

And it was in those same Genesis verses that we read for the first time these amazing words: "So God created man in his own image, in the image of God created he him; male and female created he them" (KJV). Scholars have debated the meaning of that sentence for centuries. But we have reason to believe that the idea of the image of God was quite specific in biblical times.

When a ruler of a vast empire wished to assert his rule in remote places from his capital city, he would have statues of himself made and set them up in those faraway places as reminders of his rule. These were the images of the king or emperor.

No analogy works 100 percent, but God, as Creator, made us to represent Him on planet Earth, a remote place in His realm. We are images of God whose task in life is to be reminders of Him to the people in our neighborhood and across the world.

What Kind of Person Am I?

This is why the Psalmist put the phrase "the image of God" into the poetic form, "a little lower than God," in the psalm. Usually we think too much of ourselves, apart from God, but this is a secularization of our humanity. But it is also possible for us, on the other hand, to think too little of ourselves and unwittingly belittle the intention God had for us in His creation. God made us, male and female, with majesty, nobility, and dignity. And He has given us the opportunity to represent Him on planet Earth.

Here then is the theological basis for ecology, for management of the materials, for uses of the products of the earth, and for halting the abuses of our planet and its vaporous environment. We are stewards of God, and we are to use the earth well. Abuse of the earth is another manifestation of our sinfulness, our falling short of God's intention.

It is in the wisdom psalms that we not only find our center, our purpose in the Word of God (Psalm 1), but we also find the meaning of our basic humanity (Psalm 8).

We will now turn more briefly to a few other psalms of the wise to gain more of the perspectives they present.

Psalm 14—When People Act the Fool

The Foolish Heart

Psalm 14 (and also Psalm 53, which may be edited from Psalm 14) presents another aspect of the wisdom writers; it is a discussion of folly. The fool in wisdom literature is not someone with a low IQ. Quite the opposite. He or she may be very bright. From the standpoint of biblical wisdom literature, a fool is a person insensitive to God, a person anesthetized to God's work and action in the world.

So when the psalm describes the fool as saying in his heart that there is no God (Psalm 14:1), the picture isn't of a simpleton— a "fool"—who is too dense to believe in God, nor is the term descriptive of an intellectual atheist—a "fool"—who thinks he's too wise to believe in God. The fool is a person who simply doesn't care if God is or not. Unfortunately, this is descriptive of many, many people who live in the "post-Christian" world.

The Fate of Fools

The second part of Psalm 14, beginning in verse 5, transports us to the time of future judgment of all who have rejected God. The Hebrew word translated "there" in verse 5 is a sudden interruption in the flow of the text. It is bold and daring.

"There" is an adverb of place; it speaks of a certain location, and that location is the presence of a God who sits in judgment. We see also that the fool has not only ignored the reality of God, he has abused the poor who are believers. In verse 5 the Psalmist pictures the fool caught in the clutches of excruciating fear. For the first time the fool will have experienced the God whom he ignored throughout his life. But now it is too late.

Psalm 78—Learning from History

Henry Ford is reported by the *Chicago Tribune* to have said, "History is more or less bunk." We can only guess what Mr. Ford might have meant by it, but this brash aphorism might well be the common view. History is bunk if we never learn from it. The fools of the future are those who have not learned lessons from the folly of the past.

The wisdom writers were very interested in history and in the lessons it presents. They were especially interested in salvation history, the record of the divine interventions and interactions in the story of Israel's experience. Psalm 78 gives us that history lesson.

The lengthier nature of this psalm (72 verses) may be intimidating, but the concept of the psalm is fairly easy to grasp. It is a psalm establishing the historical framework in which the tribe of Judah, and particularly the family of David, came to prominence in Israel. This psalm is a testimony for the royal house of David, Israel's greatest king (see verses 68–72).

But the psalm is also replete with warnings against disobedience to God or being forgetful of His mercies. The first of these comes in verses 9–11: The people of Ephraim did not keep the covenant of God, they did not walk in His law, and they forgot His works and His wonders.

Time after time, the Lord graciously worked in the lives of His people for their good, and on one occasion after another His people rejected His law, rebuffed His love, and spurned His presence.

But now the psalm speaks of a new king on the throne of Israel—King David. As we move toward the end of the psalm, we find no word of judgment or warning—only blessing. Yet, only a fool could read the entire psalm and not see that it is full of warning.

After all, if David or one of his descendants turned their backs on God and acted the way the people had in the past, they would suffer the judgments their foolish ancestors had suffered already.

History is bunk . . . only to fools!

Psalm 119—A Tapestry of the Word

Psalm 119 is the longest psalm in the Bible, the longest single chapter in the Bible, and one of the most ornate poems in all Scripture. One look at this psalm will tell the informed reader that this is a psalm of the wise. It has all the markings of care, craftsmanship, and focus. Here are twenty-two sections of eight verses each, totaling 176 verses, all centering on the nature and value of the Word of God. Each verse has one of the words that is used to describe Scripture. These words include terms such as "word," "statutes," "law," "commandments," "precepts," "testimony," "faithfulness," and "ordinances."

Psalm 119 is a grand acrostic. There are several other acrostics in the Bible, but this is the one on the largest scale. In the Hebrew text of this psalm, each verse begins with a word whose first letter is in alphabetical order. But there are eight verses for each letter. This means, for example, that each verse in the *Mem* section (verses 97–104) has a word at the beginning whose first letter is the Hebrew letter *mem*.

Now, imagine attempting to construct something like this in English. Don't worry about the letters we use infrequently, particularly the X. Think merely in terms of common letters. Think of writing eight couplets, each having a word beginning with A, then eight with B, and so on. Imagine writing a poem in this way that has sense, flow, and continuity; development, rhythm, and passion; and figurative language and creative expression that would sustain for nearly two hundred verses. The artistry of this psalm stretches our imaginations.

The Hebrew text of the psalm is simply exquisite. It is a monumental achievement of human creativity and endurance—a loving tribute to the significance of the Word of God.

And it is beautiful. Read just the *Mem* section (verses 97–104). These verses focus on a person who loves the Word of God. He is like the person in Psalm 1, whose meditation is in the Law of God day and night. Through the study of the Word of God, the wise man becomes wiser than his enemies, wiser than his teachers, even wiser than the ancients (verses 98–100).

But there isn't just intellectual activity involved. There is also the practical expression of wisdom. The wise person has turned from evil to the law of God. As he reads these words, he finds them to be sweeter than honey (verses 101–103).

The problem Psalm 119 presents to us is its sheer length. You might want to read it over the course of about a month, reading each eight-verse segment on a separate day. Then, as you ponder thoughtfully the words, you will be drawn into the study of the Word of God that this Psalmist rhapsodizes.

Psalm 139—His Wondrous Knowledge

You Have Searched Me and Known Me

We conclude this lesson with one more of the psalms of the wise, and this is one of the most profound. This is a psalm displaying the intimate knowledge of and relationship with the believer.

The psalm consists of six movements, and it will be helpful to keep these in mind as you read the psalm:

- The Lord knows us, the people of God, in a wondrous way (verses 1–6).
- The Lord is present with us wherever we may be (verses 7–12).
- The Lord has formed us with wonder and skill (verses 13–16).
- The Lord's thoughts are beyond our comprehension (verses 17–18).
- We are enemies to those who oppose the Lord (verses 19–22).

- Our desire is to mirror the character of the Lord (verses 23–24).

Let Me Go?

Now, what are we to make of all this? Most readers of this psalm take it positively. Most readers would conclude that the Lord's comprehensive knowledge of them is a tremendous encouragement in all of life.

But there are also those who read this psalm in a different and hostile way. God, in their view, is the hound of heaven, and no matter how hard they try, they cannot escape Him.

He Is with Me

In my own view, this psalm is to be read in a positive way. It speaks of the omniscient (all-knowing) and omnipresent (everywhere-present) nature of God. But it does not do so abstractly. God's knowledge of us is intimate and dynamic; His presence is a pursuit, but it is a loving and not a hostile chase.

The psalm points us back to the words of the covenant language God used with Moses in the passage describing the revelation of His name, Yahweh (Exodus 2:22–3:15). One of the central teachings of God to Moses then was the promise, "Certainly I will be with you" (Exodus 3:12, NASB1995). From there my mind flies forward to the departing words of the resurrected Jesus as He is ascending to His Father from the Mount of Olives: "And surely I am with you always, to the very end of the age" (Matthew 28:20, NIV).

With God's words to Moses on one hand and the words of Jesus to His followers on the other, we can now return to this psalm and see it as the working out of the promise of the Divine Presence.

What wonderful words these are: the Lord is with us!

In Summary
There are many psalms that share a point of view with the wisdom writings in the Hebrew Bible of Proverbs, Job, and Ecclesiastes. These psalms of the wise use distinctive language, present recurring contrasts, and share similar interests. They focus on God as Creator, God as Judge, and God as Present. These psalms also have a strong interest in the Word of God, the primary source of our understanding of the only wise God.

The Apostle Paul, with years of travel and ministry behind him, understood well the power of the Scriptures in the life of a Christian. In writing to Timothy, his protégé in the Gospel, he said, "But as for you, continue in what you have learned and have firmly believed, knowing from whom you learned it and how from childhood you have been acquainted with the sacred writings, *which are able to make you wise* for salvation through faith in Christ Jesus" (2 Timothy 3:14–15, ESV; italics added).

Search me, O God, and know my heart: try me, and know my thoughts. See if there be some wicked way in me, and lead me in the way everlasting. Amen.

PSALM 1; PSALM 119:1-8

Blessed is the one . . . whose delight is in the law of the LORD**, and who meditates on his law day and night.**

—Psalm 1:1–2, NIV

Blessed are those . . . who seek him with their whole heart.

—Psalm 119:2, ESV

One Sunday, our pastor emphasized the importance of having a daily quiet time. "The book of Psalms is a great place to start," he said. *Not much of a challenge,* I think. *I've been reading psalms since I was a child.*

"Sometimes I only read a verse or two a day," he added.

Oh.

"When I slow down and let the Scriptures soak in, God shows me how to pray. It's not about how many verses you read. It's about listening."

I squirmed in my seat. Lately my morning prayers had felt like busywork. I connected with God in my head but not always in my heart. If my prayers didn't reach my heart, how could they possibly reach His?

The next morning, I opened my old Bible and turned to Psalm 1. *Lord, show me how to fall in love with You again, through the psalms,* I prayed. Reminding myself to slow down, I copied a verse in my journal with a purple pen. A royal color. To honor God's Word.

As if the Lord were writing with a golden pen, He drew me to certain verses. Then He connected my mind with my heart and showed me how to pray the psalms for people I love. My prayer time grew sweeter because I finally invited God to join me.

—*Julie Garmon*

Notes

Notes

Psalms of Trust

Lord, You are my shepherd; You make me lie down in green pastures. You lead me beside still waters. AMEN.

A Sense of Trust

The psalms help us express our deepest sense of trust in the Lord's protective care. And there is probably no other place where we can get this feeling more than in the psalms of trust. These are the psalms that renew our confidence in the goodness of God, in His mercy, and in His interest in us. These are the psalms that urge confident faith and robust belief. They are also the psalms that provide shelter, comfort, and even a sense of coziness in the nestling arms of God.

In this lesson we will examine some of the psalms of trust, and we will begin with the hands-down favorite, Psalm 23. Then we will look more briefly at some others, including Psalms 27, 31, 32, 46, and 73.

A Context of Lament

You will remember from lesson 3 that the pattern of the psalms of pain was somewhat complex, containing the following elements:

- An opening cry ("O my God!")
- The lament of pain (using three pronouns): I am hurting; You do not care; they are winning

- A confession of trust
- The petition (using three verbs): Hear me! Save me! Punish them!
- A vow of praise

In the psalms for this lesson there is often a bold declaration of trust in the Lord that is followed occasionally by very strong language of lament. This declaration is called the "confession of trust." Here the Psalmist states his true and deeply felt belief system. And here the Psalmist asserts in strong, sometimes beautiful language his faith in God.

Occasionally, the confession of trust is so finely developed within a larger psalm of lament that the confession of trust might exist on its own as an independent psalm. This means from the point of view of the forms of the psalms, the psalms of trust may be considered a subcategory of the psalms of pain.

Psalm 23 is such a psalm of trust.

Psalm 23—My Shepherd

The Lord Is My Shepherd

Without question, Psalm 23 is one of the most loved of all the passages in the Bible. And rightly so! This choice little poem depicts the mystery and beauty of the relationship God has with His people. The psalm gives us a daring comparison— God is called a shepherd and His people are called sheep.

To Call God Shepherd

For most of us in the Western world, the idea of shepherding is something from another planet. Though serious farmers who rely on working the land and raising livestock are a vital part of our economy and food supply, there are also those who take a much less serious approach to farming.

Certainly, they do a great deal of work with their animals, perhaps supervising breeding, aiding in birth, tending illnesses, and butchering for meat. But, for them, the animals are something they care for as a small part of our lives. It is a hobby, not a livelihood. They are neither farmers nor shepherds in the deepest, truest sense of the terms.

The True Shepherd

A real shepherd has his whole life taken up with his flock. A shepherd is no dilettante. And for him, shepherding is a vocation, not an avocation.

An elderly man told his grandson stories of his years as a shepherd in a remote area in Canada. He told the boy about being alone with the sheep day after day and month after month. His only break would come every six months when he picked up his supplies. It was not the life for just anyone; it required a dedication and commitment that would be too much for many people. But this man was a shepherd; his life was the sheep.

God is our shepherd. His life is His sheep.

Psalm 23 has two parts. Verses 1–4 describe the shepherding image in a more literal manner; verses 5–6 describe the shepherding image in more figurative terms (verse 5) and look ahead to a future time when the Psalmist would "dwell in the house of the LORD forever" (verse 6, NIV).

I Shall Not Want

The theme of Psalm 23 says it all: "The LORD is my shepherd; I shall not want [need]" (verse 1, KJV). This sentence speaks of the ongoing relationship God has with His people. It is a relationship of person, time, care, and protection. In the world of the Old Testament, this is a stunning image. The shepherd meets the needs of his sheep in a variety of ways, providing them with food and water, touch and care, protection and comfort.

The most significant provision of the shepherd, however, is his presence. The words of verse 4, "I fear no evil, for You are with me" (NASB), are touching and are adopted from the language of covenant, now applied in the motif of sheep and shepherd.

A Table before Me

Some readers have difficulty with the language at the beginning of verse 5 because it seems to go in a different direction from the shepherding idea of verses 1–3. But it can be argued that the shepherd motif does carry on through to the end of the psalm. It is just that in verse 5 we encounter the use of hyperbole—deliberate exaggeration for effect.

Verse 5 pictures the sheep as being treated like guests at a banquet given by a gracious host. The table is the pasture, but the Psalmist compares it to a banquet table loaded with food. And to complete the picture, the Psalmist sees himself eating "in the presence of my enemies" (NIV), though they are not allowed to participate. All they can do is salivate; they are not the ones eating tonight!

But that isn't all—the provision of water is so bountiful it is like a wine goblet that is filled to the point of overflowing. And the use of olive oil to treat a scratch is likened to placing olive oil on the forehead of a traveler to refresh him from the heat of the day.

In the House of the Lord

The usual hunters or predators of sheep are wolves and dogs. But we're told that the sheep of the Good Shepherd are chased by goodness and mercy! The verb translated "shall follow" in verse 6 is a technical term for the pursuit of prey by a hunting animal. "Surely goodness and mercy shall follow me all the days of my life" (KJV).

And when this life is over, the Psalmist says with confidence, "I will dwell in the house of the LORD forever" (NIV). In the image of shepherd and sheep, the phrase "the house of the LORD" relates to the sheepfold, the ultimate place of safety. Even people who have never seen a sheep find this psalm to be beautiful, for in it we discover in an unusual manner whole new dimensions of the relationship we may have with our God.

Psalm 27—My Light and My Salvation

If the Twenty-Third Psalm is the universal favorite, Psalm 27 is probably on most people's "top forty" list. Psalm 27 has some exquisite lines of poetry, even though its structure is more complex than some psalms. This psalm can be outlined this way:

- The Psalmist states his unflinching confidence in the Lord (verses 1–3).
- The Psalmist desires to behold the beauty of the Lord (verses 4–5).
- The Psalmist declares his intention to praise God for his deliverance (verse 6).
- The Psalmist petitions the Lord for a sense of His presence (verses 7–10).
- The Psalmist prays to the Lord for protection from his enemies (verses 11–13).
- The Psalmist gives instruction to wait on the Lord (verse 14).

Light and Salvation

One of the features in the poetry of the psalms is the practice we call hendiadys (hen-DIE-uh-diss). This is a term meaning "one through two," in which one concept is expressed through two words. "Light and salvation" form an interesting example. We have had many occurrences of hendiadys in the psalms we've studied. Psalm 23 speaks of "goodness and mercy" pursuing the believer in verse 6. These are not really two entities, but the use of two words to express one idea—the supreme goodness of God.

In the same way, "light and salvation" in Psalm 27:1 does not present two separate ideas, as though God first is thought of as light and then is thought of as salvation. The words go together. As light to a person in darkness, and as salvation to a person in distress, so God is to the needy believer: He is our complete deliverance.

The Lord's Beauty

Among the loveliest expressions in this entire psalm is the sentiment expressed in verse 4, "One thing have I desired of the LORD . . . that I may dwell in the house of the LORD all the days of my life, to *behold the beauty of the LORD* . . ." (KJV, italics added).

At a Christian retreat for college students, one particularly beautiful day ended with a campfire and a time of reflection and sharing. Several of the students spoke of the lovely things they had seen that day as they had enjoyed the natural wonders around them. Suddenly, one of the students realized that a young woman nearby was blind and the lavish descriptions of beauty might make her feel left out.

But the blind young woman reassured them as she explained that their descriptions of the beauty of nature helped her imagine what it was like. "But," she said, "I know that you also have to see a very great deal that is not pretty or beautiful. Much of what each of you see is really ugly. As for me, I have never seen a thing. Someday, though, when I use my eyes for the very first time, it will be to see the beauty of the Lord." Each in their own way, the blind young woman and the Psalmist shared a marvelous hope.

Thy Face, O Lord

We have noted above that the psalms of trust are subdivisions of the psalms of pain. By this we mean that the larger form of a psalm of lament has a confession of trust within it that sometimes is separated into a psalm on its own. Psalm 27 is primarily a song of trust, but in verse 9 we have a petition: "Do not hide Your face from me" (NASB). This is the language of lament; the psalm here expresses hurt, even though, for the most part, it transcends pain.

It is helpful to understand this because some people have difficulty visualizing the tranquility of Psalm 23. They feel that it isn't like that in real life, that psalms like these present a picture that is too blissful. Yet this petition in the heart of Psalm 27 helps us strike the right balance—even though the Psalmist speaks with such bold confidence in the Lord in the early part of the psalm, he still is flooded with feelings of anxiety. In this way, the psalms speak of life the way it really is. We just have to be sure that we are reading them correctly.

My Father and My Mother

Certainly the words of verse 10 speak of life as it is. The Bible is not sentimental; it presents life. The Bible does not gloss over evil; it exposes it. And the Bible does not pretend there is no hurt in life. Rather, the words of Scripture show how a follower of God may endure the hurt, transcend the pain, and defeat the enemy.

There are few psychological pains more haunting for a child than to be abandoned by a parent who simply walks out on his or her children. But the Psalmist writes, "Although my father and my mother have abandoned me, yet the LORD will take me up [adopt me as His child]" (AMP). God is both Father and Mother to the abandoned, and He is friend to all.

Wait on the Lord

The final words of Psalm 27 are an instruction to others. Since the Psalmist has experienced such full deliverance from trouble in his relationship with the Lord, his is an authentic voice when he urges others to trust in Him as well: "Wait for the LORD; be strong and take heart and wait for the LORD" (verse 14, NIV). To wait for the Lord is not to be passive or inactive, and it certainly is not to give up. Waiting on the Lord is a dynamic exercise of faithful confidence. In his book *If You Want to Walk on Water You've Got to Get Out of the Boat*, John Ortberg wrote, "Waiting on the Lord is a confident, disciplined, expectant, active, sometimes painful clinging to God." How much better off most of us would be if, instead of plunging headlong into a situation, we would back off and wait for the Lord's guidance.

Psalm 31—My Rock and My Fortress

Psalm 31 is really a psalm of pain. It is a classic lament, with expressions of personal distress (verse 11), being forgotten by God (verse 12), and being in trouble because of one's enemies (verse 13).

In the midst of stress, however, this psalm of pain becomes a psalm of trust. That is, the trust motif of this psalm is unusually striking. This is why it is included here.

My Strong Rock

Arguably, the strongest, most central words in this psalm of trust are "For you are my rock and my fortress; and for your name's sake you lead me and guide me" (verse 3, ESV).

In Psalm 27 we discovered a feature of Hebrew style where two synonyms are linked closely to convey a single idea between them. We called this hendiadys. The words of Psalm 27:1, "my light and my salvation," refer to one concept rather than to two separate ones.

Similarly in Psalm 31, the words "my rock and my fortress" do not refer to two means of protection to be found in the Lord. They work together to convey one idea. This might be translated "my strong fortress" or "my great rock." When the poet speaks of God as his Rock in this psalm, it is not just that God is a stone, but He is a massive, solid formation—a secure defense. Had the Psalmist known about Gibraltar, he might well have said, "Yes. That's it. God to me is something like Gibraltar."

It is helpful for us to see the variety of images that the various writers use to describe God in the psalms. No one image will do. The image of God as Shepherd is one of the finest, as we experienced in Psalm 23. But the image of God as Shepherd is strengthened as we think of Him also as Rock. The rock image speaks of strength, permanence, majesty, and stability. The assertion of God as Rock is one of the oldest images in the music of ancient Israel. The term appears more than twenty times in the book of Psalms as a reference to God.

Rock of Faith

You will remember that Jesus made a wonderful pun on the name of Simon. He said, "And I also say to you that you are *Peter*, and upon this rock I will build My church" (Matthew 16:18, NASB; italics added). The Greek word for "Peter" is *petros*, meaning a little rock. The Greek word for "rock" is *petra*, meaning a massive rock ledge. And as Jesus spoke these words, doubtless it was with a gesture to the immense sheer cliff face behind him at Banias, in biblical Caesarea Philippi, a rocky site used for pagan worship from prehistoric times. With a rock behind him that denotes all the folly of paganism, Jesus spoke of the rock of faith—faith in Jesus, the Son of the living God.

Most certainly, our God is a massive Gibraltar of strength to the Christian.

Psalm 32—My Hiding Place

A Sinner Forgiven

Psalm 32, like Psalm 31, is not strictly speaking a psalm of trust. While there are differences of opinion, many scholars believe this psalm was written by David and is the result of his confession of sin concerning Bathsheba and Uriah. We have in this psalm the writer's profound statement of gratitude to God for forgiveness from sin. The psalm begins with a pronouncement of benediction: "Blessed is the one whose transgression is forgiven, whose sin is covered" (verse 1, ESV).

Then as we read on, the Psalmist admits that when he was hiding his sin, he was a man beside himself. He was ill, sleepless, tormented. He felt so drawn out that it was as though his bodily moisture was all drained from him, as though he were an outcast in the desert in the heat of summer (verses 3–4). Because of unconfessed sin, the Psalmist was a tortured man, but then when he acknowledged and confessed his sin, God forgave him! It was then the Psalmist experienced the overwhelming grace of God and was able to confess his trust (verses 5–6).

A Confession of Trust

It is in the words of verse 7 that we find the great trust element as the Psalmist writes, "You are my hiding place; you will protect me from trouble and surround me with songs of deliverance" (NIV).

My Hiding Place

The superscription preceding this psalm associates it with David, and we know that a great deal of his adult life was spent in hiding. He had been a fugitive from Saul for years, living the life of an outlaw with the sentence of death over his head. He never knew when he lay down to sleep at night whether his hiding place would be discovered by morning. At times he was not even able to trust his own men.

As a fugitive on the run, he might find a crevasse in a mountainside in which to hide. In the inner recesses there would be shelter from the heat of the day and the winds of night. And in this hiding place he could feel relatively safe.

These experiences enabled David to picture God as his hiding place. In God's protective care, he could lean back, stretch out, drop his guard, and relax in safety. And so may we!

Songs of Deliverance

Now comes the unexpected. Not only does the Psalmist find God to be a place of refuge and a protection from the evil all around him, but also when he nestles close to the divine presence, he begins to hear music—"songs of deliverance" (NASB). There was no sweeter music then or now than the divine assurance that we are safe and secure in the center of God's love.

In Daddy's Lap

On a radio program, a Christian psychologist answered an inquiry from a hurting single parent. A father had written to say that he was doing his best to be both father and mother to his little daughter after his wife had died. But a problem had developed that had him stymied.

His young school-aged daughter had begun to suck her thumb, something she had not done for years. He was concerned for her, lest she be teased at school.

The psychologist made a suggestion. She said that the father was likely working long hours, then he would pick up his daughter from her after-school day care and hurry home to fix dinner. After dinner there was the usual busyness and then bedtime.

The psychologist suggested that when father and daughter arrived home, they first settle down into a chair with him cuddling her on his lap. This way, they had time to talk, but even more important, by touching and loving her, the little girl would feel the security she had missed since her mother died. The therapist was quite confident this would correct the problem that concerned the father.

Close to the Father

This is a marvelous picture of the Christian believer in the sheltering arms of the Father above. As we move close to

Him, we will not only feel His presence but also might hear His song.

Psalm 46—My Help in Trouble

Psalm 46 is classified as one of the psalms of the sons of Korah. The Korahites were Levites who were involved in Temple music. In fact they were composers of worship music for Temple use. Psalm 46 is one of their jewels. This psalm is through and through a psalm of trust.

Unreserved Confidence

Psalm 46 presents a faith in God that can be described as unreserved confidence. There is an awesome majesty in the opening words: "God is our refuge and strength, a very present help in trouble. Therefore we will not fear though the earth gives way, though the mountains be moved into the heart of the sea, though its waters roar and foam, though the mountains tremble at its swelling. *Selah*" (verses 1–3, ESV). This is an unusual progression, with the very worst coming first (the end of the earth) and the least awful coming at the end (the shaking of the mountains). Yet there is a sense in which the least awful is the most likely and, hence, may be the truer indicator of faith in God.

The Presence of God

A second factor in this psalm of trust is the affirmation of God's presence with his people. The setting of this psalm may be prophetic, even eschatological. It is a psalm speaking of the end of time, one of many in the book of Psalms. The psalm exults not only in the defeat of the enemies of God and the establishment of the city of God with an abundant river, but it also speaks of the pleasure and confidence of the Psalmist, who affirms, "The LORD of hosts is with us; the God of Jacob is our refuge" (verse 7, KJV).

In these words, the Psalmist shares a common prophetic vista. The little book of Zephaniah, for example, ends in words very similar to this verse (Zephaniah 3:14–17). Twice in those verses the prophet speaks of the presence of the Lord in the midst of His people (verses 15, 17).

The Shekinah

When the prophets and the Psalmists speak of the coming presence of the Lord with His people, they build upon the theology of the presence of God in the holy Temple. This is referred to as the Shekinah glory. The Hebrew verb *shakan* means "to dwell" or "to reside." The first residing of the Lord with His people was in the Tabernacle in the wilderness. Then, much later His glory overshadowed the Temple in Jerusalem.

Even with this sense of His presence, however, there was the hope for something more—a more tangible sense of God's presence.

The Incarnation

The great surprise and central truth of the Gospel is that God came to dwell with people in the person of Jesus. The opening words of the Gospel of John attest to this: "And the Word was made flesh, and dwelt among us" (John 1:14, KJV). The Greek verb translated "dwelt," *skenoāo*, is the same as the Hebrew *shakan*. In His incarnation, Jesus came to dwell with His people for a time, and our hope is in the future when He will come again.

Peace and Majesty

The last section of Psalm 46 (verses 8–11) looks ahead to that time when there will be no more war. The final battle has been won, and God now rules over all the earth as King of kings and Lord of lords. At last, in a world long weary with war, there will come lasting peace. Peace in Scripture is far more than the end of hostilities. Rather, it is the gift of God that sets everything straight. Only with the presence of God with His people will full peace, *shalom*, be realized.

Our Refuge

The real meaning for us, as well as for those who first heard these words, is that the God who will accomplish all these things in the future is our refuge in the present: "The LORD Almighty is with us; the God of Jacob is our fortress" (verse 11, NIV).

This verse is repeated from verse 7; the two verses serve as a refrain in the psalm. With this refrain, the priests, during Temple worship, make the pronouncement that the future has meaning in our present.

The very God who will consummate the ages, and the very God who created all things, is the same God who offers Himself in our living as a personal refuge from the assaults of this present world.

We have now come full circle with a rereading of verse 1, "God is our refuge and strength, a very present help in trouble" (KJV).

The good news for Christians today is that the awesome God of creation, the One who at some future time will end all wars and bring lasting peace, is with us now in the daily nitty-gritty of our lives, not only as our refuge but also as our help. Amazing grace!

In Summary

That which makes the psalms of trust so special to us is the confidence we gain in the person of our God—our Refuge, our Strength! This is why when we come to the psalms of trust, we feel as if we have come home.

And we have come home to the One who is our Shepherd, our light and salvation, our strong rock, our hiding place, our help in times of trouble.

As another psalm puts it, "My flesh and my heart may fail, but God is the strength of my heart and my portion forever" (Psalm 73:26, NASB).

We have come home to God!

Thank You, Lord, for being with me; thank You
for being my refuge. AMEN.

PSALM 25

Guide me in your truth . . .

—Psalm 25:5, NIV

Since I've been starting each morning by reading a psalm or two, I've been amazed how often the Psalmist's words are exactly what I needed to hear that day! Recently, I had a tough decision to make, in which all the choices had serious drawbacks. I woke up with anxiety and uncertainty stabbing me in the chest. My marker was at Psalm 25, and as I began reading it aloud, certain phrases seemed meant just for me. "Show me your ways, Lord, teach me your paths. Guide me in your truth and teach me . . ." (verses 4–5, NIV).

Then came blessed assurances: ". . . He instructs sinners in his ways. He guides the humble in what is right and teaches them his way. All the ways of the Lord are loving and faithful . . . He will instruct them in the ways they should choose" (verses 8–12, NIV).

What a healing balm for the fearful ache in my chest! I carried verse 15 in my heart all day: "My eyes are ever on the Lord, for only he will release my feet from the snare." Near the end of the day, an alternative I hadn't thought of occurred to me, and I was able to make a truly freeing decision. You probably have some choices to make today. Maybe reading Psalm 25 aloud will help you too.

—*Marilyn Morgan Helleberg*

Notes

Notes

Psalms of Nature

◆————————————◆

*Lord, cleanse me of secret and presumptuous sins; let them
not dominate my life and character. Help me to live
an upright life, innocent of great transgression.* AMEN.

Discovering Nature

The Psalmists, like poets everywhere, were fascinated by
nature. They were captivated by things that grow, by the
mysteries of life, and by the discovery of wonder. And they
were especially enthralled with the beauty and expanse of the
heavens. You might be familiar with these words, filled with
amazement and wonder, expressed by the Psalmist when he
looked up at the expanse of the heavens and wrote, "When I
consider Your heavens, the work of Your fingers, the moon
and the stars, which You have set in place; what is man that
You think of him, and a son of man that You are concerned
about him?" (Psalm 8:3–4, NASB). But we can look other
places besides the night sky to develop a sense of wonder.
Sometimes it may be something practically underfoot.

Cracks in the Driveway

What do you do when you have a driveway in need of repair?
Let's say there are several cracks in the concrete, and some
adventuresome blades of grass have found their home in

those tiny crevices. Most of us pragmatic folks would react to this intrusion with weed killers, garden tools, or anything else handy.

But a poet looks at all of life through a different set of lenses. The poet might wander around the drive, stoop down, and observe the sprigs of grass that are growing here and there in the midst of the drive. Then his eyes might wander over to a bare spot in the lawn. And this would remind him of the widening bald spot on his head. He might then gaze out at two English walnut trees of approximately equal size and note that one has a significantly larger number of nuts forming than the other. From grass in his drive to the bald spot on his head to nuts on a tree, the poet interacts with the wonder and mystery that fills his life. In it all he constantly probes for meaning.

And if the poet is a Christian, all that he discovers in his world takes him to the mystery of the divine, to the consideration of God. He isn't a pantheist who sees God as everything. But neither is he a secularist who has no thought for God at all. Rather, in the world around him he senses that God has been here, that the Creator has left His mark. Our poet is like a sleuth, mentally dusting things in the world about him, sensing the whorls of divine fingerprints where another might not even think to look.

There are some things that have changed little over the centuries, and among those is the mind and heart of a poet. This is why the psalms of nature have so much meaning for us today.

Psalm 19—God's World, God's Word

Psalm 19 begins in the heavens, moves to the Scripture, and ends in the human heart. The psalm has three distinct sections. For this lesson, we are particularly concerned with the first six verses, but we wish to see, too, how these verses fit into the psalm as a whole. Here is an outline of the psalm:

- God's creation displays His glory (verses 1–6).
- God's Word expresses His grace (verses 7–10).
- God's people respond to His truth (verses 11–14).

The Heavens and God's Glory

As in Psalm 8, the writer of Psalm 19 looks to the heavens. But his responses to what he sees here are dramatically different from those expressed in Psalm 8. His view of the heavens in Psalm 8 left him awestruck and feeling insignificant and lonely. Only the revelation of his true significance in God's purpose restored him (see lesson 4).

But here the Psalmist's thoughts are filled with rapture, and he writes, "The heavens declare the glory of God, and the sky above proclaims his handiwork" (verse 1, ESV). The Hebrew word for "glory" (*kabod*) may seem somewhat strange in its meaning. Basically, it means "heaviness." The term describes weight, significance, presence. When we consider the heavens above, fields and sea below, tiny creatures or behemoths, birds or beasts, flowers or minerals (sprigs of grass in cracks on the drive), there is in all of them an expression of the glory of God. That is, in His creation, God has left the sense of His presence.

Psalm 19 says that this message is universal. It goes from day to day, from night to night. It extends to the end of the world. The message of God's glory is seen everywhere (verses 2–6).

In verses 4–5 the Psalmist finds himself particularly enchanted by the sun. Certainly, the sun can be viewed as a great reflection of God's glory. The Psalmist's language is colorful as he compares the sun to a bridegroom or a runner. All of life on earth is dependent in some way on the sun; how appropriate that the sun is used as the principal dancer in the ballet of the heavens.

Something of Himself

What God does and what He creates is not God, but God has left traces of Himself in all of His works. This phenomenon is explained by another Hebrew word that is sometimes used in this context. This is the word *hokma*, which is usually translated "wisdom." As with *kabod*, or glory, so *hokma* is something in creation that speaks of the Creator. For example, Proverbs 3:19 reads, "By wisdom [*hokma*] the LORD laid the earth's foundations, by understanding he set the heavens in place [*hokma*]" (NIV).

God has made the heavens and the earth, and all within them, to speak of His glory, to show forth His wisdom. The wise person responds to God when he or she confronts the creation.

When "Where" Is Not There

One of the verses in Psalm 19 raises a question. Here are the words of verse 3 in the King James Version: "*There is* no speech nor language, *where* their voice is not heard."

You will notice three words set in italics here, as is done in the King James Version. The translators of the KJV had a standard practice that is helpful for us once we understand it. When a word was lacking that the translators felt would assist in making the verse clearer to the English reader, they might add that word. Yet these translators realized that when they added words, they might in fact be in error. So they indicated these added words by the use of italics. Unfortunately, though, today we use italics to give emphasis, not for clarification.

It was not the intention of the translators to emphasize these words because *there* and *where* are not really in the original text. The verse in Hebrew actually reads, "No speech, no language, their voice is not heard," which the New International Version closely echoes with its translation: "They have no speech, they use no words; no sound is heard from them."

Not in Language

This is a significant point. It is not the intention of this verse to say that the message of creation is heard in every speech and language (though the idea of cross-cultural communication is not ruled out). Rather, the idea being expressed is that the message of creation is not a verbal message. It is real but isn't achieved through human speech. There is no speech or language in creation that we can hear.

People speak of the singing of the stars, but that is just a figure of speech. People might describe the wind sighing, leaves whispering, a brook babbling, a waterfall roaring, all of which are poetic personification but obviously not literal. While there is a message for us in God's creation, it is nonverbal. And this means there is a frightful potential for misinterpretation.

Confusion

Unfortunately, humankind has a lengthy record of misinterpreting the message of creation. In nearly every place and time, people have looked at the creature and confused it with the Creator. This is the source of all kinds of pagan idolatry; it is a confusion of product with Producer. It is like viewing a painting and not thinking of the artist. It is like touring a house and not remembering the architect, and like listening to a concerto and not considering the composer. To look at the heavens and not give any thought to God is to spurn reality.

Confession

But when we rightly see and interpret the message of nature, we know that all creation can only be understood as a demonstration of the existence of the Creator. The message of the psalm is true; it is just that a lot of people have treated it falsely.

The Word in Words

In this lesson, we are focusing on the responses of the Psalmists to nature—the creation of God. Psalm 19 has three sections, as we have noted previously. Only the first section relates directly to the concept of nature. Here is a brief summary of the rest of the psalm.

The heart of the psalm (verses 6–8) focuses on the Word of God, and in a way resembles certain passages we have already discovered in lesson 4 (see discussion on Psalms 1 and 119).

Since the revelation of God in creation is nonverbal, it has certain limitations. It is possible, for example, to view the creation of God and accept the idea that there is an all-powerful, all-wise, all-intelligent Creator—a true God who is resplendent in majesty.

But we cannot independently discover from creation the true significance concerning the love of God, the wrath of God, the grace of God, or anything else about the way He personally reveals Himself to us. We need words to comprehend God in a true sense. And for that reason, the focus on nature and creation in verses 1–6 is the prelude to the heart of the psalm, which turns our attention to the importance, beauty, authority, and desirability of the Torah, the Word of God. Bible teachers usually label the revelation of God through His Word as "general revelation." God's revealing of Himself through His written Word is a form of "special revelation."

The Word in Response

Psalm 19 now moves from the Word of God in verses 7–10 to the people of God and their responses to His message in the Word (verses 11–14). In these verses the Psalmist writes of the awareness of sin in his life, of his hope that God will act to free him from sin and its power, and of his desire to be a person who will think and act in line with God's instructions.

What a psalm this is! Its lyric poetry can scarcely be surpassed, and its message can hardly be equaled. Further, its closing benediction has been a prayer that has lifted the hearts of the people of God across the centuries: "Let the words of my mouth and the meditation of my heart be acceptable in your sight, O LORD, my rock and my redeemer" (19:14, ESV). Yes, it is a psalm of nature, but even more, it is a psalm of the Torah—the Word of God.

Psalm 65—The Song of Creation

As we have seen, Psalm 19 describes the present work of creation in the display of the glory of God. On the other hand, Psalm 65 is a predictive poem that points forward to the end of time and describes the renovation of creation under the rule of the great King. But not only will all aspects of creation be renovated, they will "shout for joy, they also sing" (verse 13, KJV).

Modern Plagues

If you've spent any time at all watching or reading the news of events around the world, it doesn't take long to encounter reports of disasters and dire situations of all kinds: war and poverty displacing thousands of people, devastating droughts, violence and other crime, endangered species, extreme weather patterns, greenhouse gases, hazardous wastes, toxic chemical spills, exploding populations.

These are the modern plagues, a rewriting of the horrors of God upon ancient Egypt. The differences between the ancient and the modern plagues are that the modern horrors are global and are induced in part by people. The biblical plagues were divine, purposeful, and redemptive. But these modern plagues are wanton, senseless, and destructive.

People of biblical faith are stimulated by the challenges of the environmental crises along with those who do not share this faith. For we share the planet; we must also share thoughtful attempts to avert its destruction. To preserve the earth is to preserve ourselves.

The Earth in Travail

But people of biblical faith should not be surprised at the turmoil and trouble that seem to hold our planet in a death grip. What we sense today may be an acceleration of the long process the Bible describes as the whole creation groaning and travailing in pain as it awaits redemption from on high (Romans 8:22).

The Year of His Goodness

All of this sets an environment in which to explore Psalm 65. For here is a poem in Scripture that looks forward to the renovation of the earth from its present trouble. This is a psalm that describes the transformation of the earth from "groaning" to "singing."

One of the keys to the interpretation of Psalm 65 is found in the phrase in verse 11, "You crown the year with your bounty" (NIV). The Hebrew text may be translated this way: "You crown the year *of* your goodness." This phrase labels that future time as the "Year of God's Goodness." This is a new term for us to relate to the biblical concept of the age to come.

Paying a Vow

A second key to understanding this psalm is found in the wording of verse 1. Psalm 65 begins with a statement that there is praise that "awaits" (NIV) or "is due to" God (ESV) but that the vow will be performed: "to you our vows will be fulfilled" (NIV). When we first begin the psalm, we wonder what this vow is and what is meant by the delay in the paying of the vow.

But as we move on through the psalm, we catch a description of great productivity in agriculture and of abundant water on fields and hills (verses 6–10). C. S. Lewis said this psalm gives us a view of rain as a vegetable might enjoy it. The "Year of God's Goodness" is a time of abundant, gracious rainfall. Now, since the Psalmist likely lived in the arid terrain that surrounded Jerusalem, he must have often wished for the refreshing and sparkling rain that would bring life to the barren Judean hills.

As we picture this, we begin to realize that the vow of the first verse is the expectation of the earth to shake off the effects of the curse that was the result of Adam's sin (Genesis 3:17) and to return to the lush splendor of the garden planted by God (Romans 8:21).

The Hills Are Alive

One day, the Psalmist predicts, there will be such luxuriance in all of nature that it will seem as though the heavens are overflowing with good things—with showers of blessing— that enrich the earth (verse 11). Our writer then colorfully pictures a lush scene in which the pastures and hills are alive with abundant crops (verse 12). Then the Psalmist closes this magnificent nature hymn with a penetrating glimpse of the natural world as God intends for it to be: "The pastures are clothed with flocks; the valleys also are covered over with corn; they shout for joy, they also sing" (verse 13, KJV).

The two instances of the pronoun "they" at the end of the verse have as their antecedents the terms "pastures" and "valleys." This is it: the vow of praise that the psalm anticipates (verse 1) is fulfilled in verse 13. This is the song of creation when the earth is finally restored to goodness. It is a garden again.

Psalm 104—What God Has Made

Back to Creation

While Psalm 19 speaks of God's glory in the present universe and Psalm 65 looks ahead to the renovation of the earth in a coming age, Psalm 104 takes us back to the beginning of creation. At the same time, the words of Psalm 104 remind us that the creative actions of God are ongoing. And as the Psalmist is caught up in the awesome wonders of God's creation, he lapses into song and praise: "I will sing to the LORD as long as I live; I will sing praise to my God while I have being" (verse 33, ESV).

Psalm 104 has an inclusio similar to the one we found in Psalm 8 in lesson 4. An inclusio is a pattern of repetition at the beginning and the ending of a section, serving as a frame for the display of the central message. Psalm 104:1 begins, "Bless the LORD, O my soul!"; the psalm ends in the same way, with a concluding "Praise the LORD!" (ESV).

Wrapped in Light

The first movement of this psalm extends from verse 2 to verse 9. Here the Psalmist describes the creative works of God in highly figurative language. This poetic reworking of the story of Genesis 1 is breathtaking. The first thing God did in creation was to call for light to appear (Genesis 1:3). Here in verses 2 and 3 we read that God covers Himself with light as with a garment. Then He stretches out the heavens like a curtain. Where the Genesis story describes the separation of waters above and below, this poem speaks of God laying beams in the chambers of the waters and making the clouds His chariot.

The figurative language of this psalm is certainly not to be interpreted as a literal description of the pattern God used in creation. In fact, it is not the intention of the writers of the Bible to tell us how God created. *How* is the mystery. Instead, they tell us that God created. The mechanics of creation are better left to God; our role is to affirm God's mighty acts of creation. With Christians since the earliest days of the church, we confess in the words of the Apostles' Creed, "I believe in God, the Father Almighty, *maker of heaven and earth*" (italics added). Our faith in God's creation is not dependent on date, means, or manner; it does center, though, on the affirmation that God is Creator.

The function of a poem is not so much to convey information as it is to share a feeling, to put words to an experience. When we read Psalm 104, we have not discovered a scientific treatise on the origin of the universe; we have found something far more wonderful. Somehow, in some mysterious way, the Psalmist is able to form into words what God may have been feeling when He created the universe.

Springs in the Valleys
The second section of the psalm, verses 10–18, moves us from the drama of creation at the beginning of time to the wonder

and beauty of nature as it continues under God's control. The descriptions in these verses are idyllic. We have here in marvelous word pictures a view of nature under God's care and direction. In fact, in the setting as described, the word *nature* seems inadequate, for it is possible to speak of nature without recognizing God in what we see. Actually, the biblical term is *creation*—a setting resplendent with lush pastures and fields, teeming with animals and birds, carpeted with forests, and watered by bubbling springs. But God's "creation" is not only a haven of beauty; it is where God is at work providing for the comfort and needs of His people—there is "wine that gladdens human hearts, oil to make their faces shine, and bread that sustains their hearts" (verse 15, NIV).

Seasons and Cycles

The third movement of the psalm, verses 19–24, speaks of the seasons of the year and the cycles of life. The actions of the sun and the moon provide light and darkness—night and day—and regulate the changing seasons. Nothing is left to chance; everything moves and functions according to God's perfect plan.

If you've ever left an ice-cold winter for balmy tropical environs, you have experienced what feels like opposite seasons separated by a ride in a plane. Some places have four very distinct seasons; some places seem to have two seasons—or what seems like 20 different mini-seasons.

But despite the variables that characterize different areas across our vast earth, one way or another, we are all aware of seasonal changes. And most everywhere the distinction is sharp between the darkness of night and the brilliance of day.

This particular part of our psalms lesson tells us that all of this comes about through the wisdom of God. Here again we confront that Hebrew word *hokma* as descriptive of the wisdom that focuses on God as the Creator.

The Sea, Ships, and Leviathan

The fourth section of Psalm 104, verses 25–30, speaks again of the sea. In the mythology of the people of the ancient Near East, the sea was regarded as a god of chaos and destruction. To the poets of the Bible, the sea became a symbol of all that was anti-God. To them the ocean was something fearful and untamed.

In the midst of the mystery of the sea, the ancients believed there were dragons—monsters of the deep. The Canaanite word for this dragon was *Lotan*, a word that became *Leviathan* in the Bible. In Canaanite mythology, Leviathan was a seven-headed fire-and-smoke-breathing dragon.

The writer of Psalm 104 has fun with these ideas. While the sea and the sea monster were regarded as malevolent gods by the people of Canaan, the Psalmist writes that the sea is tranquil and the sea monster is harmless. This movement of the psalm begins with these words: "Here is the sea, great and wide, which teems with creatures innumerable, living things both small and great" (verse 25, ESV).

For the Psalmist, the message is clear. God, in His creative wisdom, is responsible for every fish and animal found in all of the world's oceans. All are creatures of God, and all serve a specific purpose in the cycles of nature.

God's Glory Forever

All of the creative wonders of God's world move the Psalmist to praise God (verses 31–35). This is the meaning of the last section of our poem. As the Psalmist reflects on the glory of nature—all that he sees in the world around him—his heart overflows with praise: "May the glory of the LORD endure forever . . . I will sing to the LORD all my life; I will sing praise to my God . . . as I rejoice in the LORD" (NIV).

There is nothing casual about the Psalmist at this point. He has a grand sense of unrestrained exuberance as he views the wonders of God's world. In this way, the writer has given us a model to follow that is especially important. Even as Christians, we have become quite blasé about our world and the technology that has transformed our way of life. It is easy for us to lose our sense of wonder and take for granted the beauty of our world. We've become almost indifferent to the realities of powerful computers we hold in the palm of our hand, vast stores of information at our fingertips, instant (and virtually free) communication across the globe, and GPS that guides us on our travels without maps or stopping to ask for directions. We have become callused to the amazing works of God in our world today.

But the Psalmist sets a standard of praise for us. We are to look at life through the unsophisticated eyes of children in whom the sense of wonder is still intact. This is what Jesus meant when He urged His followers to be like little children. We are prone in our praying to do a lot of asking but little praising. But we will be enriched by taking a page out of the Psalmist's book, who in another place wrote, "Praise the LORD! Praise the name of the LORD; praise Him, you servants of the LORD . . . Praise the LORD, for the LORD is good; sing praises to His name, for it is lovely" (Psalm 135:1, 3, NASB).

Psalm 148—Let Everything Praise the Lord

The Psalmists view creation from a number of different vantage points. But here in Psalm 148, creation is identified not only as the work of God but also as a source of special praise to Him.

In this psalm the writer issues the call for all of God's creation to join together in a mighty hymn of praise to Him. This is an inclusive call: the heavens (verse 1); angels (verse 2); sun, moon, and stars (verse 3); the highest heavens (verse 4); fire, hail, snow, and wind (verse 8); mountains and trees (verse 9); wild beasts, cattle, and birds (verse 10); rulers, people, and judges (verse 11); and young men, young women, and children (verse 12).

Throughout the psalm we find a recurrence of the Hebrew word *hallelujah*. In this word we have an enthusiastic and excited response to the reality of God and His goodness. It means to be excitedly boastful in the Lord, to find in the Lord God of Scripture our basic reasons for being.

Then the Psalmist stretches to lofty heights as he writes, "Let them praise the name of the LORD: for his name alone is excellent; his glory is above the earth and heaven" (verse 13, KJV).

In Summary

The psalms of nature share with poetry the world over a special feeling about both the simple and the majestic things that make up our world—those things we tend so easily to take for granted. As we look through the lenses of the ancient poets, we catch the excitement of their strong attraction to nature, God's handiwork. And we find ourselves staggered by the idea that we are a part, along with God's entire universe, of a grand choir that is offering a great hymn of praise to the One who created us all.

In the word that is so much a part of Psalm 148: *hallelujah!*

Lord, the stormy wind fulfills Your Word; the fruitful trees and cedars praise You. I praise You too! AMEN.

PSALM 19

The heavens tell of the glory of God; and their expanse declares the work of His hands.

—Psalm 19:1, NASB

One of my summer jobs as a college student was working in beautiful Glacier National Park, Montana. After our tasks were completed, the other employees and I often sat in front of our dorm discussing various topics.

On this particular day we talked about whether there is a God. Being the only professing Christian in the group, I tried desperately to think of an argument that would convince the group once and for all that there is a God. But everything I came up with was refuted.

Finally, a quiet girl beside me spoke up shyly. "Who do we thank for all this?"

We followed the sweep of her arm to the meadow of yellow and blue wildflowers and a bubbling stream as clear as liquid glass. Behind the meadow, as far as we could see, ran a string of towering, craggy mountains frosted with creamy, white snow and dotted with pine-scented evergreens.

   Nobody said a word. Nature had spoken on behalf of its Maker!

—*Shari Myers Smith*

Notes

Notes

Psalms of the King

◆————————————————————◆

*Lord, You are my defense, and the Holy One of
Israel is my king.* AMEN.

Readers of the book of Psalms have always been
intrigued by those psalms that center on the person of
the king. These are sometimes called "royal psalms."
They provoke an unusual interest because they seem to flow
from David or Solomon as king to God as King, and they
seem as well to look forward to the coming time of Jesus as
King. These psalms are among the most difficult to interpret
because of this complexity in reference to varied kings. But
they are also among the most rewarding and present some of
the richest ideas.

An Example—Psalm 89

Psalm 89 is a splendid example of the psalms of the King. It
is a poetic reenactment of God's covenant with David, first
given in 2 Samuel 7:8–17 (see Psalm 89:3–4). But in speaking of "David my servant" and in exalting him as a human
model, we are also reminded that the true king of Israel is God
Himself (verse 18, KJV)—"the Holy One of Israel is our king."
The present-day Christian can see that, ultimately, this psalm

seems to speak of Jesus as being the King who will be higher than all the kings of the earth (verse 27).

In this lesson we will be looking closely at several of the psalms of the King. As we read them, we should keep in mind that the idea of kingship in the psalms is complex:

- David, or his heir, is the king of Israel because of the great covenant promise of God in 2 Samuel 7. Often these psalms of the King celebrate David, or his son Solomon, in grandiose terms. The extravagance of language serves two purposes: first, to praise the king in the family line of David; and second, to look beyond David to One greater than he.
- God (Yahweh) is the King of kings, the ultimate sovereign of the universe. This means that a king of Israel is only a local ruler under the Great King.
- Seen through Christian eyes, Jesus the Messiah is the eagerly anticipated coming King in the psalms of the King. He is the ultimate fulfillment of God's promise to David— Jesus is David's greater son and is David's Lord (Psalm 110:1; Matthew 22:41–46).

Psalm 2—God's King

Psalm 2 is perhaps the most complex of the psalms of the King. New Testament writers were particularly fond of it because they saw in it incontrovertible predictions of the Messiah Jesus (compare Psalm 2:1–2 with Acts 4:25–28; Psalm 2:7 with Acts 13:33; Psalm 2:8–9 with Revelation 2:26–27).

But before we focus on the messianic expectations in this psalm, we need to center our attention on a human king,

God's anointed. The psalm begins with reference to God's covenant with the House of David (2 Samuel 7:14).

A Coronation Song

Psalm 2 was a coronation hymn for the royal House of David. As each successive heir of the family of David was anointed king, this psalm was used as a part of the rites of his installation. The words of the poem seem to carry a direct reference to God's promise through Nathan to David and his heirs (2 Samuel 7:8–17).

With the coronation of each new king, surrounding enemy nations seized on this event as an opportunity to put pressure on Israel and possibly even launch an armed attack. Yet the writer of Psalm 2 affirms God's intention to stand by His promise to maintain a Davidic heir on Israel's throne. In fact, the psalm writer pictures as laughable the attempt of pagan kings to overthrow the Lord's anointed (verse 4).

God's assertion through the words of the Psalmist is clear: "Yet have I set my king upon my holy hill of Zion" (verse 6, KJV). God can be counted on; His promises are firm. The writer of 2 Samuel quotes God as saying, "I will be to him a father, and he shall be to me a son" (7:14, ESV). And here in this psalm is God's great affirmation: "You are my son; today I have become your father" (verse 7, NIV). (Some translations capitalize "son," which we'll see echoed in a New Testament quote a few paragraphs below.) Each successive son of David was to be adopted by God as His "son," a gracious mark of relationship between the earthly king and the King of kings.

Then the Psalmist goes on to admonish the other kings of the earth to submit to God's anointed king in Jerusalem ("Kiss the Son," 2:12, NASB), even as they come to serve the Lord (2:11).

So when we read Psalm 2 in its historical setting, we find a poem that celebrates the rule of God on earth that is realized through Israel's David and his successors.

In Praise of the Son

But applying the psalm to David and his successors fails to exhaust its meaning. Ultimately, the Christian sees Jesus in Psalm 2. A critical examination of this psalm leads us to think of a future fulfillment, and the New Testament's use of the psalm identifies that future as being fulfilled in the Lord Jesus Christ (see again Acts 4:25–28 and 13:33).

So when we read Psalm 2 as prophecy of the future, not just as a contemporary coronation hymn, we find that not only are there three movements to it, but as Christians looking back, we see each of the three movements may also be read as corresponding to a member of the Trinity.

The Laughter of God

Psalm 2:1–6 forms the first movement of this poem. Here in picture language, we see on the one hand a righteous king functioning under God's authority with the nations of the world and their rulers rising up in rebellion against the king and against God. As we have observed, the complexities of this psalm are enormous. And while the Psalmist isn't likely to have foreseen such a time of rebellion, the early Christians came to view this as a messianic psalm—one that looked ahead to the coming of Jesus and the Kingdom of God. As we have seen, this psalm is quoted several times in the New Testament. Luke makes a direct reference to it when he quotes from Paul's sermon, "He has fulfilled to us their children by raising Jesus, as also it is written in the second Psalm, '*You are my Son, today I have begotten you*'" (Acts 13:33, ESV; italics added).

Many interpreters believe the words of this psalm refer to the end of time as we know it when Jesus will return again. Without attempting to catalog mysterious events, we have references to the battle of Armageddon where "the nations conspire" and the "kings of the earth rise up . . . against the LORD" (verses 1–2, NIV). But their efforts and rebellion are futile. The Psalmist colorfully describes the scene: "He who sits in the heavens laughs, the Lord scoffs at them" (verse 4, NASB).

You Are My Son

In this second movement of the psalm, we have the exact words quoted in Acts 13:33. Here the Son receives the grand affirmation of the Father: "You are my Son; today I have begotten you. Ask of me, and I will make the nations your heritage, and the ends of the earth your possession" (verses 7–8, ESV). These words remind us of the Father's affirmation at Jesus's baptism: "And lo a voice from heaven, saying, This is my beloved Son, in whom I am well pleased" (Matthew 3:17, KJV; see also 2 Peter 1:17). And in the book of Revelation, we're told that the Son is given all power to overcome any and all who oppose Him (see Revelation 2:27; 6:15–17; 19:11–21).

A Warning and a Blessing

Psalm 2 concludes with a warning and a blessing. The leaders and rulers are warned against doing anything that would block the ultimate rule of God over the earth. They are warned against frustrating the will of the Son. And then the Psalmist writes, "Blessed are all they that put their trust in him" (verse 12, KJV).

And for Us Today?

This psalm points back to the rule of the House of David in Jerusalem and forward to the rule of Jesus, the Suffering Servant-King, over the earth. But, we may wonder, what does it have to say to us today? Psalms such as this one give us stability, meaning, and hope.

First, Psalm 2 assures us of the rule of God in all times, including the twenty-first century. We can have complete confidence that no president, prime minister, monarch, dictator, or despot can frustrate the ultimate purposes of God. Here is a basis for our feelings of stability.

Second, the psalm assures us of the purpose of God in history. Unlike many views of history that were prevalent in biblical times, and unlike the views of history held by many people today, the Bible presents history that is moving steadily in a God-ordered direction. There is nothing capricious about the direction, and its culmination is in God of history as humankind moves steadily toward the Lord's eternal purpose. Here is a basis for our sense of meaning.

Third, the psalm excites us with the promise of a future day in which there will be an end to the arrogance and sinfulness in people. Irrespective as to how hopeless and gloomy the present scene may be, our hope is in God, the Creator of our vast universe and everything in it.

Psalm 24—The King of Glory

The Sovereign Lord

Psalm 24 begins with a grand affirmation that God is King. He is the Creator of the earth and all that is in it (verses 1–2). The words "The earth is the LORD's, and all it contains, the world, and those who live in it. For He has founded it upon the seas and established it upon the rivers" (NASB) assert His rule. These words could well introduce a worship service. When we come to the worship of God, we are approaching majesty, and when we enter God's house to worship Him, we come before a King.

We learned earlier that reference to "the seas" (verse 2) speaks of the ancient Canaanite cultural setting of Israel's poetry. The sea is a symbol of chaotic and evil forces. The intent of the Psalmist is not to convey the idea that the world is floating on a bed of seas. Rather, he picks up on Canaanite imagery as he says that God as King has formed an ordered world upon seas and rivers that are symbolic of the subdued powers of chaos and evil. The foes of God are subdued; the restless powers are no longer a threat. We will explore this further in our discussion of Psalm 93.

The Holy Place

When people come to the worship of God, they are approaching the throne of majesty. The question that the second part of Psalm 24 (verses 3–6, NASB) presents is haunting: "Who may ascend onto the hill of the Lord? And who may stand in His holy place?"

There are two answers to this question. One is immediate and relative; the other is distant and absolute. First, these words can be understood as referring to relative righteousness. In the time that the psalm was written, the understanding would be that those who have avoided gross sin, who have a heart for God, and whose actions have been motivated by purity of heart could approach the holy place before a holy God in worship. But even so, only the high priest could enter the Holy of Holies in the Temple.

Who May Stand in His Holy Place?

Many people today have lost the concept of sin as it is presented in the Bible. While it's not a topic people in general are comfortable discussing, and it is not something that Christians should dwell upon or obsess about, sin does exist.

We are not perfect, even when our intentions are largely good and we are generally good people. And the truth is that a person who is just "a little bad" is not good enough. Despite popular belief, God does not keep a record of the good things we do and weigh them against the bad things to decide if we enter heaven.

Rather, God knew long ago that none of us is perfect—which is the only way we'd be good enough to be in His presence. This is made clear in another psalm that says, "There is no one who does good, not even one" (14:3, NIV). The Apostle Paul echoed this same truth when he wrote the Christians in Rome that "all have sinned and fall short of the glory of God"

(Romans 3:23, ESV). And so as we read these verses of Psalm 24 in the light of God's absolute demands, we must come to the devastating conclusion that no one can ascend the hill of the Lord and stand in the holy place.

But wait! For the Christian, the story doesn't end there. While it is true that we have all sinned and failed to measure up to God's standard of righteousness, it is also true "that, while we were yet sinners, Christ died for us" (Romans 5:8, KJV), and through His death and Resurrection, we have become children of God. Through Christ, we can "come boldly unto the throne of grace, that we may obtain mercy, and find grace to help in time of need" (Hebrews 4:16, KJV).

In writing to the Christians in Galatia, Paul worded it this way: "So you are no longer a slave, but God's child; and since you are his child, God has made you also an heir" (Galatians 4:7, NIV). What a glorious heritage!

The King of Glory

Verses 7–10 of Psalm 24 present a majestic pageantry with antiphonal choirs. The Kingship of God is the central theme of this closing movement of the psalm. We can feel the joy and triumph of this song of proclamation:

Lift up your heads, you gates;
  be lifted up, you ancient doors,
   that the King of glory may come in.
Who is this King of glory?
  The LORD strong and mighty,
   the LORD mighty in battle.
Lift up your heads, you gates;

lift them up, you ancient doors,
   that the King of glory may come in.
Who is he, this King of glory?
   The Lord Almighty—
   he is the King of glory.
—Psalm 24:7–10, NIV

In this magnificent liturgical exchange, we catch a definite military tone. The Lord God, the King of glory, the Creator of the universe, has overcome all the chaotic forces of evil and is firmly entrenched as the righteous and holy God. And it is this God who loved the world so much that He gave His only Son that we might have life (John 3:16).

Psalm 45—The King of Love

A Song of Lovers
One of the most unusual of the kingly psalms is this love poem. There are some affinities between this psalm and the biblical book we call the Song of Songs or the Song of Solomon. Psalm 45 is a love song that is associated with the wedding of a king and his bride. It also has prophetic overtones that point to the Suffering Servant-King, the Lord Jesus Christ.

A Detailed Tapestry
The psalm is notoriously difficult to interpret in its details, but as we examine it in broad outline, it begins to come together. It is not unlike an exceedingly ornate tapestry. At first glance it is easy to become lost in the intricacies of design and detail. But then as we step back and view the tapestry as a whole, we

become aware of the big picture. This is the way we will look at Psalm 45.

The psalm has four broad sections:
- The beauty of the king (verses 1–5)
- The reign of the king (verses 6–9)
- The bride of the king (verses 10–15)
- The praise of the king (verses 16–17)

The Beauty of the King

Usually we think of a wedding in terms of the bride—her beauty and radiance. All eyes are on the bride as she begins processing down the aisle of the church toward her groom. She is the center of attention.

But in this royal wedding song, the major attention is first directed toward the groom. Note the Psalmist's introduction as he gives this description of the groom-king: "You are the most excellent of men and your lips have been anointed with grace, since God has blessed you forever" (verse 2, NIV). The king is pictured in these words as a man of beauty and grace whom "God has blessed." The reference to the king's beauty is not physical but to the quality of his character. He is a man whose words are kind and gracious because he cares for and is concerned with the welfare and feelings of his people.

This attribute of the groom-king calls to mind the importance of our words. As Christians, our conversation should be graceful and uplifting—not critical, cutting, or judgmental. It is tragically easy to become careless and thoughtless about the way we talk to and about other people. And yet it is through our words that we give expression to our inner thoughts.

Two thousand years ago the writer of the book of James described our need well when he said, "Who is wise and understanding among you? By his good conduct let him show his works in the meekness of wisdom. But the wisdom from above is first pure, *then peaceable, gentle,* open to reason, full of mercy and good fruits [deeds], impartial and sincere" (James 3:13, 17, ESV; italics added).

In verses 3, 4, and 5 of the psalm, the majestic quality of the groom-king is pictured in terms of his military abilities with the sword and sharp arrows. But the writer suggests in verse 4 that the purpose of the king's preparedness is for truth, meekness [humility], and righteousness.

The Reign of the King

In verses 6–9 of the psalm, the poet lauds the king as God's anointed and speaks of the king's throne as being the earthly symbol of God's throne. The grandeur of the Psalmist's words in these verses moves us out of the twenty-first century and into the time of this groom-king who loved righteousness and hated evil (verse 4).

As we ponder the words of this psalm, we are drawn, as so often happens, in two directions. First, we see in this psalm a royal figure in the history of ancient Israel. This might be the wedding day of a great Davidic king such as Solomon or Hezekiah. We can only speculate and extrapolate because nothing about this psalm dates it. But we do know that whoever he was, his people saw him to be a true king chosen by God in line with God's promises as found in 2 Samuel 7. As such we can understand the enthusiasm of the poet as he sees the king and his bride on their wedding day.

The Bride of the King

In verses 10–15, the scene moves to the bride. Again, the poet's description is lavish. The bride is exquisitely dressed. The Psalmist writes that her "clothing is interwoven with gold" (verse 13, NASB). The picture here is of a noble young woman whose attire symbolizes a person of rich character and worth. The pageantry in the wedding scene is awesome. At the same time in verses 11 and 12, we catch a hint of the bride's sense of aloneness as she moves from a familiar past to an unfamiliar future.

If you watched one of the royal weddings, such as that of Prince William and Kate Middleton, you know the television screen was filled with pomp and circumstance. The splendid uniforms of the prince and his attendants, the gorgeous gowns worn by the bride and her attendants, and the guards standing at frozen attention give a glimpse of the wedding described in this psalm.

Commitment to One Another

We also see in these verses that as the bride moves from the old into the new, she can be assured of the king's adoration. And with that commitment, the poet writes, "Bow to him" (verse 11, ESV). The word used in the King James Version, "worship," might be familiar from its use in the Anglican *Book of Common Prayer*'s wedding liturgy, "The Form of Solemnization of Matrimony": "I thee worship." In marriage, it reminds us of Paul's admonition to be "subject to one another out of reverence for Christ."

Though in the broader context of our faith, the words *bow to* or *worship* can be taken literally, in the context of marriage vows, the words are used to mean "honor" (verse 11, NIV). The word refers to a celebration of the highest idea in monogamous marriage: finding in the other person one's highest good and to give to that person one's all.

In marriage, we surrender to each other in a bonding for life—a fulfillment of the words of the Genesis writer, "Therefore shall a man leave his father and his mother, and shall cleave unto [be united with] his wife: and they shall be one flesh" (2:24, KJV). It is the giving of ourselves without reservation and the acceptance of the other without hesitation.

The Praise of the King
In the final words of the psalm, attention is directed back to the groom-king. Here we see the glad responses of the people who have witnessed the wedding even as we catch the word of promise for the future in the mention of the king's heirs.

Another King
As we have seen, Psalm 45 is a wedding poem or song. Yet the people in ancient Judaism and early Christianity saw it also as a psalm pointing toward the coming Messiah. The writer of the book of Hebrews makes the Christian connection clear as he writes, "But of the Son he says, 'Your throne, O God, is forever and ever, the scepter of uprightness is the scepter of your kingdom. You have loved righteousness and hated wickedness;

therefore God, your God, has anointed you with the oil of gladness beyond your companions'" (Hebrews 1:8–9, ESV).

Another Wedding

But there's more. The early Church and Christians down through the centuries have connected Psalm 45 with Christ and the Church—a prefiguring of the union of Christ and His Church at the end of time as we know it. In strange (to us) and awesome metaphorical language, the writer of the book of Revelation refers to this scene as "the marriage of the Lamb" (19:7, ESV). This setting in Revelation 19:1–10 is, like Psalm 45, a time of great celebration and victory. The Greek word *alleluia*—praise God—is used repeatedly in the King James Version.

The writer of the book of Revelation describes the scene this way: "Then I heard what sounded like a great multitude, like the roar of rushing waters and like loud peals of thunder, shouting: 'Hallelujah! For our Lord God Almighty reigns. Let us rejoice and be glad and give him glory! For the wedding of the Lamb has come, and his bride has made herself ready'" (19:6–7, NIV).

Admittedly, it is difficult for us as Western Christians of the twenty-first century to fit ourselves into such scenes—with past kings and a future event described in picture language. But in this psalm, as in all of the royal psalms of the King, we cannot help but be caught up in a grand expression of alleluia to God for His guidance on a day-to-day basis and for our eternal hope.

Now, we will take a brief look at three more psalms of the King.

Psalm 72—The King of Righteousness

A Coronation Prayer

Psalm 72 is the expression of the highest ideal of kingship in the ancient Near East. It is the biblical model of what a king ought to be. This psalm is described as a coronation hymn for Solomon. God's loftiest desires for Israel's kings are summarized here. The principal theme is righteousness.

The king of Israel was intended to be a model of the commands of sacred Scripture. He was to be the epitome of righteousness. In observing the life of the king, the people would have the pattern and standard for their own lives.

Come See the Best

Needless to say, only with the vaguest approximation, and only for the shortest time, were the ideals of this psalm ever realized in any of Israel's kings. Their nobility did not bring about complete faithfulness to God. But we may see nobility of purpose at least in the vision they had for themselves on their best of days.

David and Solomon, Jehoshaphat, Hezekiah, Uzziah, and Josiah were the best kings, but none of them was perfect. At their best they showed what a king might be, but by their weaknesses they exemplified far too often what kings more normally came to be.

Come See Jesus

And so it is that in every king we find ourselves on a quest for one better, for one who finally realizes the ideal.

As modern-day Christians, when we read Psalm 72 with Jesus as its ultimate fulfillment, we see the following development:

- Jesus, the righteous King, institutes the rule of peace (verses 1–4).
- Jesus, the righteous King, showers blessings upon His people (verses 5–7).
- Jesus, the righteous King, extends His rule throughout the earth (verses 8–11).
- Jesus, the righteous King, delivers the needy and the poor from all their troubles (verses 12–15).
- Jesus, the righteous King, provides plenty for all the earth (verse 16; recall Psalm 65 in lesson 6).
- Jesus, the righteous King, is blessed forever (verse 17).
- Jesus, the righteous King, gives glory to the Father (verses 18–19).

This marvelous psalm closes with words of praise we might well echo at the close of every day: "Blessed be the LORD God, the God of Israel, who alone works wonders. And blessed be His glorious name forever; and may the whole earth be filled with His glory. Amen and Amen" (72:18–19, NASB).

Psalm 93—The King of Might

This is a short psalm of praise to God as the majestic King of the universe—the One in complete charge. For our brief study, it is broken down as follows:

- The rule of God as King is majestic and His realm is stable and secure (verse 1).
- The rule and realm of God are eternal (verse 2).

- The rule of God is certain—never wavering (verses 3–4).
- The rule of God is true and sacred (verse 5).

In these few words the Psalmist pictures a Creator-God who is mighty, all powerful, unchangeable, and secure. The forces of nature are under His control—the floods, the churning waves, and the turbulent seas are all subservient to Him.

The ancient reader would have seen something here that we can easily miss, for the Psalmist, in addition to offering praise to Israel's God, was launching an attack against corrupt Baal worship. While Baal, the supreme Canaanite deity, is not mentioned here, nor is Yamm, the Canaanite god of the sea, the description in verses 3–4 has its roots in ancient mythology. As the Canaanite story goes, Baal and Yamm were locked in mortal combat. In the midst of the ferocious mythological battle, Baal emerged as the victor but only after receiving a mortal wound. He was revived by a consort, but he was always threatened by attack from the angry sea. This is one reason the ancients regarded the sea as being evil.

The Psalmist, then, is asserting here that the Lord God of Israel is mightier than any other gods—the "many waters" and "the mighty waves of the sea" are under His control. And what was true of those ancient Canaanite gods is also true of our twenty-first-century idols—power, money, social position, and politics.

Psalm 98—The King of Joy

Joy to the World

In this psalm the poet breaks out in unrestrained praise to the God whose "right hand and his holy arm" (ESV) brought

Him victory over the chaotic forces of evil and who continues to watch over Israel with righteousness, love, and justice. In response to the Lord's benefits, His people are urged to "make a joyful noise to the LORD, all the earth" (ESV).

When Isaac Watts wrote the words to his beloved Christmas carol "Joy to the World," he used the words of Psalm 98 in a slightly different form. Through our experience with these psalms of the King, we can see why Watts believed that this psalm anticipated the coming reign of Jesus Christ. And that anticipation has filled Christians in all times with an exuberant and overflowing joy. Celebration is the proper mood for the people of God, for He is indeed the King of joy.

In Summary

These royal psalms of the King in the Hebrew Bible are complex and at times difficult to understand because they range from direct descriptions of historical kings in ancient Israel to the Creator-God in heaven to the expectation of the future King. It is also difficult for most of us in the Western world to think in terms of a king or kingdoms or supreme rulers.

Yet the truths of God that flow through these psalms as we've studied them are as meaningful now as when they were first written in their Oriental setting. We worship a Creator-God who is in ultimate control not only of planet earth but also of the entire universe. At the same time, He is a caring and loving God—the God who gave His Son that we might have life.

As we reflect on that truth and on these psalms of the King, we, too, can join with Isaac Watts in singing, "Joy to the world, the Lord is come; let earth receive her king!"

Lord, I sing unto You a new song; for You have done marvelous things. You are holy, and You have the victory. AMEN.

SINGING THE PSALMS

The Bible strongly associates the psalms with music. Many of the psalms refer to musical instruments being used to praise God, and many instruct us to sing. Psalms formed the hymnal for the early church—as we read elsewhere in this study, Mark 14:26 tells us that Jesus and His disciples sang a hymn at their Passover gathering we know as the Last Supper.

From the earliest days of the church, Christians have gathered to sing. You probably have sung the psalms without even realizing it. Many writers of now-familiar hymns took one step back from singing the actual psalms with common melodies and paraphrased them some-what to make them both more singable and more pleasing to the ear. Isaac Watts is probably the most famous of these hymn writers. Some of Watts's best-known hymns that grew from this move-ment are listed here:

"Our God, Our Help in Ages Past"
(Psalm 90)

"Joy to the World" (Psalm 98)

"Jesus Shall Reign Where'er the Sun" (Psalm 72)

"My Shepherd Will Supply My Need" (Psalm 23)

Other examples of paraphrased psalms set to hymns include "The King of Love My Shepherd Is" (also based on Psalm 23), "Hiding in Thee" (Psalm 61), "Glorious Things of Thee Are Spoken" (Psalm 87), "All People That on Earth Do Dwell (Psalm 100), "Bringing in the Sheaves" (Psalm 126), "O Worship the King" (Psalm 104), and, of course, Martin Luther's "A Mighty Fortress Is Our God" (Psalm 46). Well over one hundred hymns—many of them still sung today—borrow from or paraphrase various psalms.

More recently, writers of praise and worship music have picked up the mantle of these hymn-writing forebears, following the Psalmist's admonition to "sing a new song." A well-known example is Martin J. Nystrom's "As the Deer" (Psalm 42), and new psalm-based songs are being written all the time.

Notes

Notes

Psalms of the Savior

Lord, thank You for being at and on my side; You are
my ever-present advocate and guide. AMEN.

F
or the Christian reader of the book of Psalms, there
is a recurring question: how do the psalms speak of
Jesus? For today's Christian, we have seen some of the
ways that the psalms speak of Jesus in the psalms of the King.
But we may have more questions than ever as we wonder how
other psalms might be thought of as referring to the Savior.

That the psalms do speak of Jesus is incontrovertible from
the vantage of the New Testament and the early Christians.
Read, for example, the report of Jesus's words to a group of
Pharisees in Matthew 22:41–46. Jesus's citation of Psalm 110:1
as a statement about Himself is thought to have been critical
to His position. Jesus specifically says that these words in the
psalms speak of the Messiah as the Lord of David, even though
the Messiah will be the son of David! In this and in numerous
other places, New Testament writers assert that the psalms
speak of, or point to, the person of Jesus the Messiah.

The quotations of several of the psalms by the New Testament
writers have led to the development of the idea of "messianic
psalms." These are psalms that are generally thought to speak
in some way to the coming of the Messiah. The listing of

messianic psalms includes Psalms 2, 8, 16, 22, 23, 24, 40, 41, 45, 68, 69, 72, 89, 102, 110, and 118. There are three problems, however, in any listing of messianic psalms.

First, this, or any similar, listing of messianic psalms includes poems that speak of Jesus in considerably different levels of specificity and clarity. Psalms 2 and 110, for example, are seen as far more directly messianic than Psalms 41 and 45. But when we list them as messianic psalms, we seem to indicate that the clarity of messianic ideas is obvious and equal. Not all the verses of even the messianic psalms speak of Jesus or speak of Him in the same manner.

Second, once we have decided a psalm is messianic, we may tend to lose any sense of the meaning of the psalm in the setting in which it was written. Psalms 8 and 22, for example, should be interpreted first in terms of the life and times of David before we ask how these psalms speak of Jesus. We may rush to find Jesus in the psalm and miss some of its original intent.

Third, by speaking of certain psalms as messianic, we limit ourselves to the messianic expectation that many other psalms also may share.

His Psalms

There is a sense in which *all* of the psalms are psalms of the Savior. Most interpreters usually tend to categorize certain psalms as messianic because they seem to speak prophetically of Jesus and are quoted by New Testament writers as being fulfilled in Him. But in our study, we've seen that we can't be that precise because many other psalms may speak of Him as well.

Here are some indicators:

- *The blessed man* in texts such as Psalms 1 and 112, for example, speaks in general ways of *any* person, man or woman, who is righteous and blessed of the Lord. But since this phrase may describe any righteous person, ultimately it speaks of the most blessed Person of all, the Lord Jesus Christ. As an experiment, go back to Psalm 1 and read the text thinking of the person as Jesus. He is the One who is altogether innocent of evil, whose life is thoroughly centered in the Torah of God, and who, like a tree, is altogether prosperous.

- *The innocent sufferer* in texts such as Psalms 3 and 4, for example, is a term used to describe the historical experiences of David and others. But these experiences are expressed in such general terms that they can be applied to any person who suffers in innocence. And since those psalms can apply to any innocent sufferer, man or woman, they apply most directly to Him, who is the ultimate expression of innocent suffering. Again, as an experiment, read Psalms 3 and 4 thinking not of David specifically, or of an innocent person generally, but of Jesus.

  Note, for example, the words of Psalm 3:3, "But You, O LORD, are a shield for me, my glory [and my honor], and the One who lifts my head" (AMP).

  It is uncanny, isn't it? Verses like this one that have such rich meaning in the life of the Psalmist work as well in describing the life of the Savior Jesus.

- *The majestic man* in texts such as Psalm 8:5–8 speaks first of man as God created him; here is man as male and female at the beginning. Then there is a sense in which these words may speak of any person who lived his or her life in covenant conformity to faith in the Lord in biblical times. Certainly the Psalmist must have thought these words applied to himself, for his expression of distress in verses 3–4 included himself. But ultimately, these words must speak of Jesus, for it is He who recovers our true humanity, a humanity that is as God intended it to be. The writer of the Epistle to the Hebrews certainly understood that Jesus was seen in Psalm 8 (see Hebrews 2:5–10).

- *The upright* in passages such as Psalms 15 and 24 may refer to any Israelite. But the reader of psalms such as these is well aware that there is really only One who fulfills these descriptions completely. Only Jesus is truly upright.

- *The king* in the psalms is a subject we developed in lesson 7. Again, when we read of the king in the psalms, we think usually first of David or one of his heirs. Then we think of God, who is the great King. But finally, we are driven to think of the future rule of Jesus as King, and the New Testament confirms this expectation.

- *The poor and needy* are less obvious categories related to the Savior, but these words are also descriptive of His life, as He identified with the helpless so He could be the helper of all. For example, Psalm 109 is not usually thought of in messianic terms. But the identification of God with the poor and the needy (verses 30–31) moves us to this idea.

- *The one who speaks in wrath* is the identification with which we are least comfortable. However, the Savior is also judge and the One who will rule with the "rod of iron" (Psalm 2:9, ESV and other versions). Imprecations—curses against enemies of God, which we have seen in several places—are ultimately the words of Jesus in judgment against the stubborn, unchanging wicked foes who resist His rule and who reject His grace.

Now, in this last lesson we will examine a few of the psalms that are generally understood to refer to the Savior Jesus in a special manner. We will not study these psalms in their entirety but will focus on the major sections in which prophecies of the Savior seem prominent.

Psalm 118—His Passion

Passover Seder

Every year Jewish people all over the world continue a tradition from their earliest experience—the celebration of the Passover. This is a marvelous time of feasting and commemorating the deliverance God worked in the lives of their ancestors in bringing them from bondage in Egypt to freedom.

A part of the liturgy of the table is the reading of several psalms. It is customary to read Psalms 113 and 114 before the dinner, and Psalms 115 through 118 when dinner is over. Each of these psalms has a special significance in the Passover tradition, but none is as impressive as Psalm 118. This is the Passover Psalm. Although it is not specified in scripture, scholars suggest that the psalm likely was one of what are called "Hallel" psalms (113–118). *Hallel* means "praise" in Hebrew. It is certainly possible Psalm 118, with its clear messianic overtones, was the psalm that Jesus and His disciples sang at the conclusion of their Passover celebration on the night of Jesus's betrayal and arrest (see Matthew 26:30 and Mark 14:26). The New Testament often quotes Psalm 118, referring to Jesus.

A Song of Suffering

In Psalm 118 we have a picture of an innocent person who is undergoing suffering but who is determined to hold steady with his trust firmly placed in the Lord (verses 5–14). Repeatedly, the Psalmist insists that despite the attacks that are launched against him, he will overcome his enemies because the Lord is with him.

A Song of Salvation

A key to this psalm and to the music of the Bible is found in verse 14. Indeed, in these words we have the central song of salvation from Israel's earliest music: "The LORD is my strength and my defense; he has become my salvation" (NIV).

Again we have an example of hendiadys in the words *strength* and *song*. It is not that the Psalmist is speaking of two different things—God is my strength/God is my song. They go together: God is my strong song. The idea is taken from the first of the psalms of the Bible, the Psalm of Moses and Miriam, just after Israel had been delivered from Egypt and the army of Pharaoh. The Exodus writer said, "Then sang Moses and the children of Israel this song unto the LORD . . . The LORD is my strength and song, and he is become my salvation" (Exodus 15:1–2, KJV).

In singing these words at Passover, the community of faith asserts a line of continuity with the past that is compelling. The same God that delivered our spiritual ancestors from

Egypt is at work in our lives today. For the Savior, these words had special poignancy, as He sang them with His disciples just before He left the shelter of the Upper Room for the place of treachery in the garden.

A Song of Confidence

Psalm 118 is also a song of great confidence in the protecting hand of God. For even as the right hand of God (God's power) delivered the people of Israel from Egypt, the Psalmist could see this same power operating in his own life (verses 15–16). And certainly Jesus experienced this same power when He left the Upper Room to confront His enemies in the garden.

A Song of Life

Jesus knew full well that He was moving steadily toward the time of His death, for this was the reason that He had been born (see Psalm 40:6–8; compare Hebrews 10:5–7). But it was the words of Psalm 118:17–18 that must have encouraged Him in His humanity during the dark hours that would lead to His passion: "I will not die, but live, and tell of the works of the LORD. The LORD has disciplined me severely, but He has not turned me over to death" (118:17–18, NASB).

While these words do not rule out death altogether, they rule out abandonment in death. Indeed, this is the same message as found in another psalm: "[For] you will not abandon me to the realm of the dead, nor will you let your faithful one see decay. You make known to me the path of life; you will fill me with joy in your presence, with eternal pleasures at your right hand" (Psalm 16:10–11, NIV).

In fact, these words from Psalm 16 form the basis for the apostolic preaching of the Resurrection of Jesus (see Acts 2:25–32; 13:35). Jesus's hope for Resurrection was in the psalms of confidence!

A Psalm of the Lord's Doing

Verses 22–24 of Psalm 118 are thought to be among the most intensely messianic verses in the Old Testament. Jesus, during the week before the Crucifixion, referred to these verses (Matthew 21:42) as did Peter in his defense before the high priest (Acts 4:11) and in his first epistle to the Christians in Asia Minor (1 Peter 2:7).

In verse 24 we have that magnificent affirmation that is quoted so often: "This is the day that the LORD has made; let us rejoice and be glad in it" (ESV). This sentence had profound meaning in the Passover hymn, even as it is a powerful affirmation for every day of our lives.

A Song of Blessing

Finally, read thoughtfully verses 25–26. These are the words sung by the crowds as Jesus entered the city of Jerusalem on Palm Sunday at the time of what we call His Triumphal Entry (see Matthew 21:9; Mark 11:9–10; Luke 13:35; John 12:13).

The Hebrew word translated "save now" is the same as the New Testament word *Hosanna*. When the crowd shouted "Hosanna," they were actually imploring Jesus to save them! This was precisely what He had come to do.

And when they shouted, "Blessed is he who comes in the name of the Lord!" (Matthew 21:9, NIV), they were unwittingly identifying Jesus as God's Promised One, the Messiah. The people may not have fully realized what they were saying, but the religious leaders knew and understood. They shouted at Jesus to stop the crowds from this blasphemy. His response is unforgettable: "I tell you that, if these should hold their peace, the stones would immediately cry out" (Luke 19:40, KJV). This tells us just how significant the words of Psalm 118 were to the Savior as He made His way to Calvary.

Psalm 22—The Death He Died

From the New Testament perspective, Psalm 22 is a superb messianic psalm. We need to remember, however, that when the Psalmist wrote these words, he was describing his own pain in the midst of some personal experience. Before this could be interpreted as a psalm of the Savior, it was the personal lament of the Psalmist's pain and agony; yet we have in these words the experience of Jesus. The very opening words of the psalm, "My God, my God, why have you forsaken me?" were among Jesus's last words on the cross before His death (Matthew 27:46, ESV). But now, let us examine the psalm more closely.

In the first eighteen verses we have an interplay between words of lament and words of trust. In this we have an elaborate development of the pattern of the psalms of pain (see lesson 3).

- Lament (verses 1–2): Why have you forsaken me?
- Trust (verses 3–5): You are holy, O God!
- Lament (verses 6–8): I am a worm; they laugh at me.
- Trust (verses 9–10): You brought me out of the womb.

- Lament (verses 11–18): Trouble is near, and there is none to help.

As we reflect on these verses knowing what we do about the life and death of Jesus, it could seem almost as though the Spirit of God dictated the language. Yet we know that isn't the case because a dictated poem like this would have had no meaning to the Psalmist. This was the Psalmist's experience long before it came to be associated with the Savior. But isn't it remarkable that the exaggerated language of the Psalmist in describing his own pain became an accurate description of Jesus's suffering?

A Song of the Cross

Now, read verses 14–18 slowly, carefully, and prayerfully. Here we have in first-person language what Jesus must have felt as He hung on the cross in the intense heat of the day—the pain, the shame, the agony, and the humiliation. In twenty-first-century comfort and culture, we find it virtually impossible to imagine the suffering or visualize the scene. Had there been a film crew present that day in Jerusalem recording every scene, capturing every sound, it could scarcely have caught a more accurate picture of what happened than is given to us in the central verses of this psalm. In this holy place in Scripture, we move in beside Him and sense His pain.

A Song of Help

As we saw in lesson 3, the psalms of pain move from lament to petition through the statement of trust in God. The Psalmist now shifts to petition in verses 19–21. As the poet calls for help and deliverance, we hear Jesus on the cross calling out to the Father—"Help me! Deliver me! Save me." But at no point does He single out His tormenters and shout, "Punish them!" Instead Jesus asks the Father to forgive those who had hurt Him.

A Song of Triumph

Psalm 22 doesn't end with the cry for help. The remaining verses are expressions of confidence that the Psalmist's petitions are heard and that God will answer. Jesus, too, had supreme confidence in His Father. In the garden Jesus had prayed, "Abba! Father! All things are possible for You; remove this cup from Me; yet not what I will, but what You will" (Mark 14:36, NASB). But while He was hanging on the cross, He did not ask that the cup of suffering be removed. Instead, He figuratively held the cup high and said, "Father, into your hands I commit my spirit!" (Luke 23:46, ESV).

As we look further at these closing verses, we note the difference between the experience of the Psalmist and Jesus. The Psalmist uttered words of praise because he was saved from death. On the other hand, Jesus in the Resurrection was saved *through* death. For this, shouts of praise have echoed through all the centuries.

◆————————————————◆

Lord, I praise You, I glorify You, I revere
You because You hear my cry. AMEN.

PSALM 22:1–18

For dogs encompass me; a company of evildoers encircles me; they have pierced my hands and feet—I can count all my bones—they stare and gloat over me; they divide my garments among them, and for my clothing they cast lots.

—Psalm 22:16–18, ESV

As a mom I learned very quickly not to let my children know when they were going to the doctor for immunizations. If I told them too early, I'd hear about it for days. Most of the time I'd tell them when we arrived at the doctor's office, because knowing about the prick and the pain to come was as painful as the prick itself.

Realizing this makes me more in awe of Jesus's sacrifice; His death for our salvation was known. Hundreds and hundreds of years before Christ's death, David wrote about it in the psalms, down to specific details such as Jesus having His hands and feet pierced and lots cast for His clothes. More than that, it was planned by His Father. Acts 2:23 (NIV) reads, "This man was handed over to you by God's deliberate plan and foreknowledge; and you, with the help of wicked men, put him to death by nailing him to the cross."

Knowing Jesus faced pain and death for my sins causes my heart to ache. Realizing that God planned it from the beginning of time and He still created man makes it even more meaningful. My children being worried about immunizations for a few days pales to our Christ knowing of His death from creation, but Jesus setting His eyes on the cross long before He walked the earth makes me love Him even more.

—*Tricia Goyer*

Notes

Notes

Acknowledgments

Scripture quotations marked (AMP) are taken from the *Amplified Bible*. Copyright © 2015 by The Lockman Foundation, La Habra, California. All rights reserved.

Scripture quotations marked (ESV) are taken from *The Holy Bible, English Standard Version*. Copyright © 2001 by Crossway Bibles, a division of Good News Publishers. Used by permission. All rights reserved.

Scripture quotations marked (KJV) are taken from the *King James Version of the Bible*.

Scripture quotations marked (NASB) are taken from the *New American Standard Bible*®. Copyright © 1960, 1971, 1977, 1995, 2020 by The Lockman Foundation. All rights reserved.

Scripture quotations marked (NIV) are taken from *The Holy Bible, New International Version*®, *NIV*®. Copyright © 1973, 1978, 1984, 2011 by Biblica, Inc. Used by permission. All rights reserved worldwide.

A Note from the Editors

We hope you enjoyed *Living with Purpose Bible Study: Psalms* published by Guideposts. For over 75 years, Guideposts, a nonprofit organization, has been driven by a vision of a world filled with hope. We aspire to be the voice of a trusted friend, a friend who makes you feel more hopeful and connected.

By making a purchase from Guideposts, you join our community in touching millions of lives, inspiring them to believe that all things are possible through faith, hope, and prayer. Your continued support allows us to provide uplifting resources to those in need. Whether through our communities, websites, apps, or publications, we inspire our audiences, bring them together, and comfort, uplift, entertain, and guide them. Visit us at guideposts.org to learn more.

We would love to hear from you. Write us at Guideposts, P.O. Box 5815, Harlan, Iowa 51593 or call us at (800) 932-2145. Did you love *Living with Purpose Bible Study: Psalms*? Leave a review for this product on guideposts.org/shop. Your feedback helps others in our community find relevant products.

Find inspiration, find faith, find Guideposts.

Shop our best sellers and favorites at
guideposts.org/shop

Or scan the QR code to go directly to our Shop